Speaking of
ABRAHAM LINCOLN

Speaking of
ABRAHAM LINCOLN

The Man and His Meaning
⁀ for Our Times ⁀

RICHARD NELSON CURRENT

University of Illinois Press

URBANA AND CHICAGO

This book is printed on acid-free paper.

Library of Congress Cataloging in Publication Data

Current, Richard Nelson.
  Speaking of Abraham Lincoln.

  Includes index.
  1. Lincoln, Abraham, 1809-1865 — Addresses, essays,
lectures.   I. Title.
E457.8.C968   1983   973.7   83-3568
ISBN 0-252-01056-6

PREFACE

THESE TALKS have something to say about both the record and the reputation of Abraham Lincoln. Through them, it is hoped, Lincoln will have something to say to the reader. They review the uses that, from time to time, various groups have made of his name and fame; they undertake to correct the story where it is inconsistent with the historical evidence; and they attempt to show the continuing relevance of Lincoln for our time. Presented over a period of more than a quarter-century, the talks — here arranged in the order of their original delivery — also reflect changes in the intellectual climate during that period (1955-82). Eight of them are brought together from scattered publications in which they have appeared. The other three are here published for the first time.

CONTENTS

〚 I 〛

Lincoln and Daniel Webster

TODAY ABRAHAM LINCOLN is well remembered — in Lincoln Day addresses and otherwise — while Daniel Webster has become by comparison almost a forgotten man. The two were not always so far apart in the memory of the American people. In 1900, when judges for the new Hall of Fame at New York University chose the greatest American of all time, George Washington was still first in the hearts of his countrymen with ninety-seven votes, and Abraham Lincoln and Daniel Webster were tied for second with ninety-six apiece.[1]

Though Webster's and Lincoln's careers overlapped, their personal acquaintance was slight and, whether as human beings or as political symbols, their differences were striking. The one was known as the Godlike Daniel and the Defender of the Constitution, but he was known also as the defender of the moneyed interest of the North and, on occasion, of the slavery interest of the South. The other was known as Honest Abe, the friend of the common people, the Great Emancipator of the slaves. The high-living Webster, with his leonine head and his stately manner, had the appearance of greatness even after his eating and drinking hab-

Address at the forty-sixth annual Lincoln's Birthday exercises of Zeta Psi fraternity, University of Illinois, Urbana-Champaign, February 12, 1955. Reprinted by permission from the *Journal of the Illinois State Historical Society*, 48 (Autumn 1955): 307-21.

its had made him paunchy. The abstemious Lincoln, with his long arms and legs and his gawky figure, so easy to caricature, always looked pretty much like what he once had been, a small-town politician from the prairies.

The dissimilarities between them could be multiplied, but it is more to the point to consider what they had in common. If Webster was a corporation lawyer, Lincoln also served as counsel for such corporations as the Illinois Central and Ohio & Mississippi railroads; and if Lincoln rode the rural circuit in his state, so did Webster in his, as a young attorney in New Hampshire. In politics Webster was a Federalist and then a Whig, Lincoln a Whig and then a Republican. Both men, as conservatives, were generally moderate and conciliatory in their approach to public issues. And Lincoln was often influenced by Webster's example and precept.

The story of their relationship divides naturally into three periods. In the first, Webster is a famous man and Lincoln a comparative nobody who admires him from afar as an orator second to none and a party leader second only to Henry Clay. In the next, Lincoln is a rising politician who tries to identify his own cause with that of the dead Webster and thus benefit from the latter's reputation. In the final phase, Lincoln himself is the great man, finding inspiration in the words of Webster as he faces the challenge of Civil War statesmanship.

[1]

During the early 1830's, while Webster in Washington engaged in verbal duels with the South Carolina nullifiers, Lincoln in New Salem followed the debates and read with special admiration the glorious Reply to Hayne, which concluded with that line once familiar to every Northern schoolboy: "Liberty *and* Union, now and forever, one and inseparable!" Then, while Webster and the Whigs in the Senate argued with President Jackson's followers over the bank question, Lincoln and the Whigs in the legislature at Vandalia echoed the argument. In 1836, when Webster was one of

2

three Whig candidates for the presidency, Lincoln and his colleagues endorsed the whole of their party's tricephalous ticket, though it was a rather forlorn campaign for Webster and the Whigs.[2]

The next year Lincoln had his first opportunity to meet the distinguished senator from Massachusetts. On a tour of the West, Webster visited Springfield, which, largely due to Lincoln's efforts, had just been made the capital of Illinois. As a local party leader, Lincoln was presumably one of the hosts at the barbecue in Porter's Grove, where Webster delighted the crowd with some of the eloquence he always seemed to have on tap. Very likely he and Lincoln had interesting things to say to one another in private conversation, but there is no record of what, if anything, they said.[3]

Four years later Webster, as secretary of state, had his hands full of applications for jobs in the foreign service, one of them submitted in Lincoln's behalf. Lincoln was then a despairing would-be bridegroom who had broken his engagement to Mary Todd. His law partner, Congressman John T. Stuart, apparently thinking a change of scenery would be good for him, wrote to the secretary of state to recommend Lincoln's appointment as chargé d'affaires in Bogotá, Colombia. No appointment ever came through. Lincoln remained in Springfield and married Miss Todd on November 4, 1842.[4]

Five years after that, Lincoln went to Washington as the lone Whig congressman from Illinois and renewed his acquaintance with Webster, now back in the Senate. According to the gossipy Washington journalist Benjamin Perley Poore, Webster remembered Lincoln as an attorney who had searched some Illinois land titles for him and had charged only ten dollars, which Webster repeatedly insisted was so small a fee that it left him still in debt to Lincoln. Senator Webster also "used occasionally to have Mr. Lincoln at one of his pleasant Saturday breakfasts, where the Western congressman's humorous illustrations of the events of the day, sparkling with spontaneous and unpremeditated wit, would give great delight to 'the solid men of Boston' assembled around the festive board."[5]

Congressman Lincoln and Senator Webster saw eye to eye on the Polk administration and the Mexican War. Both of these Whigs, along with others of their party, denounced the war and condemned the president for having started it. In a House speech of July 27, 1848, which he revised as a campaign pamphlet, Lincoln insisted that the Whigs were nevertheless patriotic. They not only had voted war supplies but also had sent their own sons to war. "Clay and Webster," he noted, "each gave a son, never to be returned."[6]

But Lincoln and Webster did not agree when it came to choosing a Whig successor to the Democrat Polk. Lincoln was an early and enthusiastic advocate of the Whig general and hero of Buena Vista, Zachary Taylor. "Our only chance is with Taylor," he wrote a friend. "I go for him, not because I think he would make a better president than Clay, but because I think he would make a better one than Polk, or Cass, or Buchanan, or any such creatures, one of whom is sure to be elected, if he is not." Lincoln went to Philadelphia to do what he could for Taylor at the national convention, and he stumped wholeheartedly for the candidate after Taylor had won the nomination. Webster, on the other hand, condemned Taylor as merely a military man with no political experience and called the nomination "not fit to be made." Only during the closing days of the campaign did he speak out for the candidate, and even then his praise was faint indeed.[7]

His term in Congress over and Taylor inaugurated, Lincoln desperately wanted a federal job as commissioner of the General Land Office. But there were four other Illinois Whigs after the job, foremost among them Justin Butterfield, a Chicagoan who had not been, like Lincoln, an early and zealous Taylorite. Lincoln became angry when he learned that Butterfield had the backing of both Webster and Clay. "It will now mortify me deeply if Gen. Taylors administration shall trample all my wishes in the dust merely to gratify these men," he wrote to a friend.[8] The man whom Clay and

Webster recommended got the job, and Lincoln never quite forgave either of his Whig heroes.

At the moment Lincoln was a thoroughly frustrated politician, the outlook for him very bleak. Within the next few years, however, Webster was to suffer a more bitter and more final frustration, dying as he missed his last chance for the presidency. And Lincoln, advancing to the goal that Webster never reached, was to make political capital out of Webster's reputation as an advocate of American solidarity and sectional compromise.

[2]

Throughout the 1850's the American people discussed with growing heat the question of slavery in the territories, and eventually they divided and went to war over it. The Compromise of 1850 had supposedly put this question to rest by leaving the people of New Mexico and Utah, the only territories whose status was still unsettled, to decide for themselves whether they should become free or slave. Clay originally introduced the compromise proposals, and both he and Webster eloquently supported them — the latter in his Seventh of March speech, in which he said Congress need not act to keep slavery out of the territories, since God had already done so by creating geographical conditions unsuited to the "peculiar institution" of the South. While Webster was execrated by the abolitionists of New England, the Compromise and its sponsors were generally approved in Illinois and the Old Northwest.

Lincoln, in his effort to rise by capitalizing upon the popularity of the Compromise, had to contend against a better-known and more influential politician from his own state — the Little Giant, Stephen A. Douglas. In 1854 Senator Douglas, the chief exponent of "popular sovereignty" in the territories, put through Congress his Kansas-Nebraska bill which extended that principle to the unorganized territory of the Louisiana Purchase, previously closed to slavery by Congress in the Missouri Compromise. Douglas thus revived the whole dangerous issue. In the Northwest a violent reaction against his Kansas-Nebraska measure led directly to the formation of the Republican party. He protested that he was carrying on in the spirit of the Compromise of 1850, but Lincoln and others contradicted him. Douglas the Democrat and Lincoln the Republican both sought votes by appealing to the memory of the departed Whig statesmen, and each claimed to be the true disciple of Webster and of Clay.

This argument had begun at least as early as the presidential campaign of 1852, when there still was a Whig party and Webster was still alive. At that time Lincoln accused Douglas of falsely crediting the Democrats with the Compromise and brazenly stealing Clay's and Webster's ideas. In 1854, after his Kansas-Nebraska Act had aroused such widespread opposition, Douglas put his own emphasis upon the bipartisan nature of the Compromise, saying it had been the work both of Whigs like Clay and Webster and of Democrats like Lewis Cass. Lincoln complained: "The Judge [Douglas] invokes against me, the memory of Clay and of Webster." Lincoln went on to say that they were great men but were on *his* side, not on Douglas's. He asked: "For what is it, that their life-long enemy, shall now make profit, by assuming to defend them against me, their life-long friend?" And he answered his own query: "The truth is that some support from whigs is now a necessity with the Judge, and for thus it is, that the names of Clay and Webster are now invoked." Again in 1856, when he was stumping for John C. Frémont, the first Republican presidential candidate, Lincoln countered Douglas by aligning himself on the side of the old Whigs. A Democratic newspaper reporter, dropping in on one of Lincoln's campaign talks at Petersburg, "heard him pronouncing, with thundering emphasis, a beautiful passage from Webster's compromise speech, and that, too, *without the quotations.*"[9]

This same contest for identification with Clay and Webster ran through the Lincoln-Douglas campaign of 1858. "It would be amusing, if·it were not disgusting, to see how quick these compromise-breakers administer on the political effects of their dead adversaries, trumping up claims never before heard of, and dividing the assets among themselves," Lincoln exclaimed in a speech at Springfield before the formal debates began. Then, in the first joint debate at Ottawa, Douglas came back at his opponent by asserting that not he but Lincoln was the compromise-breaker. "Lincoln went to work to dissolve the Old Line Whig party," Douglas resumed in the second debate at Freeport. "Clay was dead, and although the sod was not yet green on his grave, this man undertook to bring into disrepute those great compromise measures of 1850, with which Clay and Webster were identified." In appearances by himself at Tremont and Carlinville, Lincoln denied Douglas's charges and repeated that he stood exactly where Clay and Webster had taken their stand. In the third joint debate at Jonesboro Douglas returned to the attack, and in the fourth at Charleston he elaborated by saying that "no sooner was the rose planted on the tomb of the Godlike Webster" than Lincoln and others tried to abolitionize the good old Whig party.[10]

To the very last — on through his defeat for the presidency in 1860 — Douglas stuck to his position that "popular sovereignty" should prevail in the territories. But Lincoln and the Republicans did *not* forever hold to *their* principle that slavery must be excluded from the territories by act of Congress. Early in 1861 Republican majorities in both houses passed, and Lincoln as president signed, laws which set up territorial governments in Colorado, Dakota, and Nevada without any prohibition of slavery. The assumption was that slavery would not go into these territories in any case; but that had been Douglas's assumption all along, as it had earlier been Webster's. Even such a Republican of Republicans as James G. Blaine afterward saw the territorial legislation of 1861 as a triumph not only for Webster but also for Douglas.[11]

Neither Webster nor Clay was individually responsible for the Compromise of 1850, for that was essentially a bipartisan achievement. Douglas himself, more than any other one man, engineered the final passage of the Compromise bills, and they were carried through by the overwhelming vote of the Democrats as well as the Whigs. The roles of Clay and Webster were afterward so much exaggerated as to become almost mythological.[12] The man who was mainly responsible for the Compromise itself was also largely responsible for the misconceptions regarding it. Douglas used the great Whig reputations in an effort to attract old Whigs to the Democratic party and prevent Lincoln from drawing them to the Republican party. Spurred on by Lincoln, he so minimized his own role in the Compromise of 1850 that he distorted history and dimmed his own reputation.

As David Donald has shown in a witty article, present-day politicians seem to think they must prove that Lincoln is on their side, and they devote much ingenuity to "getting right with Lincoln."[13] A hundred years ago politicians thought they had to have the late great Whigs with them, and Lincoln for one spent a good deal of effort in getting right with Clay and Webster.

[3]

After Lincoln's "rise to power" he still found occasions to recall the time when he had been an aspiring but obscure politician and Webster a man of influence and prestige. There seemed to be in Lincoln at least a trace of bitterness left over from the days when Webster, along with Clay, had helped to frustrate his fond hopes for a government job. Possibly he had his old disappointment in mind when as president, in a cabinet conversation, he agreed that Clay and Webster had been "hard and selfish leaders, whose private personal ambition had contributed to the ruin of their party."[14]

Lincoln, however, did not let these feelings affect his disposal of patronage. Generously he allowed Webster's son Fletcher to remain in the office of surveyor of the port of Boston as a holdover from the Buchanan administration. And when Fletcher organized a Massachusetts regiment "which," as Lincoln wrote to his secretary of war, "Hon. Daniel Webster's old friends very much wish to get into the service," Lincoln gave his approval to its being mustered in. Colonel Webster took his regiment to war and was killed at the second battle of Bull Run.[15]

As he faced the duties of war leader, Lincoln must have been troubled by recollections of his years in Congress when he had joined Webster in criticizing the Mexican War. When in 1863 Lincoln exiled Clement L. Vallandigham, the Ohio Peace Democrat, Vallandigham's sympathizers reminded Lincoln of his own remarks in the days when he had been an antiwar Whig. Now Lincoln drew a distinction between wartime remarks made before mass meetings and those made inside the halls of Congress. He denied that he had ever opposed the Mexican War in popular discussions. In saying this he was less than candid, and he probably satisfied his conscience no better than he satisfied the followers of Vallandigham. As James G. Randall has said, Lincoln would have resented it if President Polk had banished a man like Webster for criticizing the war with Mexico, whether in or out of Congress.[16]

But President Lincoln also had happier and less troublesome reminders of Webster — such as the anecdotes he told about him. One of these stories ran through Lincoln's mind on a bright May morning in 1862 as he watched a parade of Negro Sunday school children in the White House yard. "Did you ever hear the story of Daniel Webster and the schoolmaster?" he asked the men around him as he stepped back from the window. He proceeded to tell how the young Daniel had been repeatedly punished by his teacher for coming to school with dirty hands. One day the teacher asked to look at them. As the boy went forward he surreptitiously licked one palm, wiped it on his pants, then exhibited it. "Daniel," said the teacher sternly, "if you will find another hand in this school-room as filthy as that, I will let you off this time." The quick-witted Daniel promptly held out his other hand. "That will do," sighed the teacher. "You may take your seat." Having concluded, Lincoln laughed as loudly as any of his hearers.[17]

Lincoln told another Webster story to Francis B. Carpenter, the portrait painter, on a spring day in 1864 as he walked with him to Brady's photographic galleries to have his picture taken. Carpenter said something about "the penalty which attached to high positions in a democratic government — the tribute those filling them were compelled to pay the public." Lincoln then observed that there were different notions about what constituted a great man. And that reminded him of Webster's visit to Springfield twenty-seven years before. As Webster arrived in town and the welcoming band and procession moved down the street, a barefoot boy pulled at the sleeve of one of the citizens and asked what all the excitement was about. "Why, Jack," was the reply, "the biggest man in the world is coming." Now there happened to live in Springfield a gigantic fat man by the name of G. Jack ran up the street to see the visitor but soon came back with a disappointed air. "Well, did you see him?" the citizen inquired. "Ye-es," said Jack, "but laws — he ain't half as big as old G."[18]

[4]

To most of his contemporaries the sonorous Webster seemed one of the supreme orators of all history, the equal of Edmund Burke and even of Demosthenes. Few considered the rather thin-voiced Lincoln worthy of comparison with him. But Horace White of the *Chicago Tribune,* after hearing a speech of Lincoln's in 1854, thought it on the whole better than Webster's best. "It lacks something of the smooth, compulsive flow which takes the intellect captive in the Websterian diction," White commented, "but it excels in the simplicity, directness and lucidity which appeal both to the intellect and to the heart." And Horace Greeley of the *New York Tribune,* who was in Lincoln's audience at Cooper Union in 1860, said he never had listened to a greater speech, though he had heard several of Webster's best.[19]

It was embarrassing for Lincoln when the master of ceremonies, introducing him at the Astor House in New York during his journey to Washington as president-elect, mentioned that on other occasions Webster and Clay had spoken in the very room where Lincoln was now to speak. Since Lincoln was saving his policy announcements for the inaugural, he really had nothing to say at this time. "I did not understand when I was brought into this room that I was brought here to make a speech," he protested. "It was not intimated to me that I was brought into the room where Daniel Webster and Henry Clay had made speeches, and where one in my position might be expected to do something like those men."[20]

In Lincoln's opinion Webster was a remarkable orator, well worth reading and rereading. Lincoln once told Henry C. Whitney, his Urbana friend on the Eighth Judicial Circuit, that Webster "had no grace of oratory, but talked excellent sense and used good language." He added that he was especially impressed by a speech he himself had heard Webster make. In it, as Lincoln remembered, Webster had said: "Politicians are not sunflowers, they do not . . . turn to their God when he sets, the same look which they turned when he rose." This quotation recurred to Lincoln after he became president and had to deal with office-seekers. He put it into the draft of a talk he was to give in Baltimore in the spring of 1864, but then in revising the speech he took the passage out.[21]

Other and more important addresses by Lincoln owed a good deal to Webster. In preparing his House Divided speech of 1858 he used the Reply to Hayne as a kind of model, and while working on his first inaugural address he again had before him that masterpiece of Webster's.

Lincoln — as Horace White observed — surpassed Webster in simplicity, directness, and lucidity. Compare the opening lines of the Reply to Hayne with Lincoln's much briefer paraphrase in the House Divided speech. "When the mariner has been tossed for many days in thick weather, and on an unknown sea, he naturally avails himself of the first pause in the storm, the earliest glance of the sun, to take his latitude, and ascertain how far the elements have driven him from his true course. Let us imitate this prudence, and, before we float farther on the waves of this debate, refer to the point from which we departed, that we may at least be able to conjecture where we now are." That is Webster. And this is

Lincoln: "If we could first know *where* we are, and *whither* we are tending, we could better judge *what* to do, and *how* to do it."[22]

On the significant issues of the Civil War, President Lincoln repeatedly spoke in Websterian echoes and acted in a Websterian spirit. On the question of slavery within the Southern states he agreed much more nearly with Webster than with the abolitionists or Radical Republicans. In his first inaugural he took precisely the position on the matter that Webster had taken in the Seventh of March speech. Each state, said Lincoln, had a right "to order and control its own domestic institutions according to its own judgment exclusively," and the Constitution required "the reclaiming of what we call fugitive slaves." In a similar vein Webster in 1850 confessed he had no plan for disposing of slavery, but he expected it to disappear in a century or so, and he was willing to support a program for colonizing freed Negroes outside the country. During the war Lincoln proposed a plan for freeing the slaves, which he originally preferred to either the Emancipation Proclamation or the Thirteenth Amendment. He expected the process to take many years and, like Webster, he favored the settling of freedmen in foreign lands.[23] Both made the cause of human freedom secondary to that of national unity.

On the questions of democracy and Union, Lincoln again and again quoted or adapted the words of Webster. The memorable phrase at Gettysburg — "of the people, by the people, for the people" — was a terse wording of what Webster, Theodore Parker, and others had variously expressed. Webster in *McCulloch* v. *Maryland* and in the Reply to Hayne said: "It is, Sir, the people's constitution, the people's government, made for the people, made by the people, and answerable to the people." The "last hopes of mankind," Webster declared in 1825, rested on the success of the Union, the American experiment in popular government. Unless that experiment succeeded and the Union was saved, Lincoln warned in 1862, we would lose "the last best, hope of earth." Physically the North and South could not separate, Webster maintained in 1850, and Lincoln did the same in 1861. To Webster the question of slavery in the territories was a "mere abstraction," and to Lincoln the question whether the seceded states had ever actually left the Union was after Appomattox a "merely pernicious abstraction."[24]

Today Lincoln and Webster deserve to be remembered together as heroes in the work of redeeming American democracy and nationality. In the words of the Lincoln biographer Albert J. Beveridge, "It was the noble passages from Webster, learned in school by Northern boys, that prepared them to respond, with arms in their hands, when Lincoln called them to support the National Government and to save the Union."[25]

NOTES

1. Claude M. Fuess, *Daniel Webster* (Boston: Little, Brown, 1930), 2:375. For Webster's reputation and his significance for our time, see also Richard N. Current, *Daniel Webster and the Rise of National Conservatism* (Boston: Little, Brown, 1955), pp. 184-202.

2. Paul M. Angle, ed., *Herndon's Life of Lincoln* (Cleveland: World, 1949), p. 386; Harry E. Pratt, *Lincoln 1809-1839* (Springfield: Illinois State Historical Library, 1941), p. 49; Albert J. Beveridge, *Abraham Lincoln, 1809-1858* (Boston: Little, Brown, 1928), 1:168, 171.

3. Fuess, *Webster,* 2:64; Pratt, *Lincoln 1809-1839*, p. 86.

4. Fuess, *Webster,* p. 94.

5. Benjamin Perley Poore in Allen T. Rice, ed., *Reminiscences of Abraham Lincoln by Distinguished Men of His Time,* 8th ed. (New York: North American, 1889), p. 222.

6. Roy P. Basler, Marion Dolores Pratt, and Lloyd A. Dunlap, eds., *The Collected Works of Abraham Lincoln* (New Brunswick, N.J.: Rutgers University Press, 1953-55), 1:515. I am indebted to Mrs. Pratt for providing from the index, then in manuscript, all references to Webster in the *Collected Works*.

7. Lincoln to Jesse Lynch, April 10, 1848, ibid., 1:463; Beveridge, *Lincoln,* 1:441-42; Current, *Webster,* pp. 154-56.

8. Beveridge, *Lincoln,* 1:487-90; Lincoln to Josiah M. Lucas, April 25, 1849, in Lincoln, *Collected Works,* 2:43-44.

9. Lincoln, *Collected Works,* 2:121-32 (Lincoln's eulogy of Clay, who died June 29, 1852), 137-38, 282, 367, 370.

10. Ibid., 2:519; 3:2-3, 61, 77, 102-3, 168-71, 270.

11. James G. Blaine, *Twenty Years of Congress: From Lincoln to Garfield* (Norwich, Conn.: Henry Bill, 1884), 1:269-72.

12. See George D. Harmon, "Douglas and the Compromise of 1850," *Journal of the Illinois State Historical Society* 21 (January 1929): 453-99; George Fort Milton, *Eve of Conflict: Stephen A. Douglas and the Needless War* (Boston: Houghton Mifflin, 1934), pp. 64-78; Frank H. Hodder, "The Authorship of the Compromise of 1850," *Mississippi Valley Historical Review* 22 (March 1936): 525-36; and especially Holman Hamilton, "Democratic Senate Leadership and the Compromise of 1850," ibid. 41 (December 1954): 403-18.

13. David Donald, "Getting Right with Lincoln," *Harper's Magazine* 202 (April 1951): 74-80.

14. John T. Morse, Jr., ed., *Diary of Gideon Welles* (Boston: Houghton Mifflin, 1911), 1:507 (entry for January 8, 1864).

15. Lincoln, *Collected Works*, 4:336, 405. For Fletcher Webster's years in Illinois, see Coleman McCampbell, "H. L. Kinney and Daniel Webster in Illinois in the 1830's," *Journal of the Illinois State Historical Society* 47 (Spring 1954): 35-44.

16. J. G. Randall, *Lincoln the President* (New York: Dodd, Mead, 1945-55), 3:266-67. Lincoln also drew the distinction that while the Whigs voted "that the war was unnecessarily and unconstitutionally begun by the President of the United States," they also voted "for all the supply measures which came up, and for all the measures in any way favorable to the officers, soldiers, and their families, who conducted the war through" (Lincoln, *Collected Works*, 4:66).

17. Francis B. Carpenter, *The Inner Life of Abraham Lincoln: Six Months at the White House* (Boston: Houghton Mifflin, 1883), pp. 130-32; Lucius E. Chittenden, *Recollections of President Lincoln and His Administration* (New York: Harper, 1891), pp. 330-34. The two accounts vary in details.

18. Carpenter, *Inner Life*, p. 37.

19. Horace White, *Lincoln in 1854* (Springfield: Illinois State Historical Society, 1908), pp. 9-11, 21-22.

20. Lincoln, *Collected Works*, 4:230-31.

21. Henry C. Whitney, *Life on the Circuit with Lincoln,* ed. Paul M. Angle (Caldwell, Idaho: Caxton, 1940), p. 497; Lincoln, *Collected Works,* 7:303.

22. *Works of Daniel Webster* (Boston: Little, Brown, 1851), 3:270; Lincoln, *Collected Works,* 2:461.

23. Webster, *Works,* 5:333, 354-55; Lincoln, *Collected Works,* 4:251. On Lincoln and emancipation see Randall, *Lincoln the President,* 2:126-50.

24. Webster, *Works,* 1:77 (Bunker Hill address, June 17, 1825: "The last hopes of mankind, therefore, rest with us; and if it should be proclaimed, that our example had become an argument against the experiment, the knell of popular liberty would be sounded throughout the earth"); 3:321 (second reply to Hayne); 5:362 (Seventh of March speech,

1850: "We could not separate the States. . . . There are natural causes that would keep and tie us together"); Lincoln, *Collected Works,* 4:259 (first inaugural: "Physically speaking, we cannot separate"); 5:537 (annual message, December 1, 1862: "We shall nobly save, or meanly lose, the last best, hope of earth"); 8:403 (last public address, April 11, 1865).

25. Beveridge, *Lincoln,* 2:131.

[II]

The Friend of Freedom

HIS HAND TREMBLED as he held the gold pen, ready to
sign. He hesitated. Before him lay the broad sheet of paper
on which was written the proclamation, complete except for his
signature.

"Now, therefore I, Abraham Lincoln . . . on this first day of
January, in the year of our Lord one thousand eight hundred and
sixty-three . . . do order and declare that all persons held as slaves
. . . are, and henceforward shall be free. . . ."

Finally, with several men about him in his office witnessing the
act, he signed, writing out his full name (rather than the usual *A.
Lincoln*). For all the care he took, his signature was noticeably un-
even and infirm.

This, he insisted, was due to no hesitation or uncertainty about
the policy he was proclaiming. For three hours he had been shak-
ing hands with the visitors who trooped into the White House
from the mud and slush of a dismal, overcast New Year's Day. His
hand was tired, swollen, hard to control.

Though, as he said, *he* had no doubt about the policy he was
confirming, others since have disagreed as to what that policy ac-

Address at the third annual Lincoln observance, Kalamazoo College, Kalamazoo, Michigan, February 9, 1957. Reprinted by permission from Richard N. Current, *The Lincoln Nobody Knows* (New York: McGraw-Hill, 1958), pp. 214-
36.

tually was. Supposedly, of course, it was emancipation. Supposedly, with the trembling movement of his pen, he prepared the way for universal freedom even if he did not strike the shackles from the millions of bondsmen all at once. But possibly he was doing the opposite of what he seemed to do. Possibly he had adopted the idea of an Emancipation Proclamation as a stratagem to delay rather than to hasten the freeing of the slaves.[1]

[1]

Some of the admirers of Lincoln, viewing the Emancipation Proclamation as the grand climax of his career, have thought of him as at heart an abolitionist, one who from early manhood had been awaiting his chance to put an end to slavery. This notion can be made to seem plausible enough if only a part of the record is revealed.

There is, for instance, the story of his second flatboat voyage down the Mississippi. He was then twenty-two. In New Orleans (the story goes) he with his companions attended a slave auction at which a "vigorous and comely" mulatto girl was being offered for sale. She was treated like a mare, the prospective bidders inspecting her up and down, pinching and feeling, and then watching while she was made to trot back and forth. To Lincoln the spectacle was so shameful that it aroused in him at once an "unconquerable hate" toward the whole institution of slavery. "If I ever get a chance to hit that thing," he swore as he walked away, "I'll hit it hard."

Lincoln perhaps took a stand for freedom as a member of the Illinois legislature in 1837, when resolutions were introduced in response to the mob murder of Elijah Lovejoy, the antislavery newspaperman of Alton. These resolutions, instead of denouncing lynch law, condemned abolitionist societies and upheld slavery within the Southern states as "sacred" by virtue of the federal Constitution. Lincoln refused to vote for the resolutions. Not only that — together with a fellow member he drew up a protest against

17

them, declaring that slavery was "founded on both injustice and bad policy."

Interesting also are his reflections on his experience of 1841, when with his friend Joshua Speed he was returning from a Kentucky visit. He made part of the trip by steamboat down the Ohio. "You may remember, as I well do," he wrote to Speed fourteen years later, "that from Louisville to the mouth of the Ohio there were, on board, ten or a dozen slaves, shackled together with irons. That sight was a continual torment to me; and I see something like it every time I touch the Ohio, or any other slave-border." Speed, having resettled in Kentucky, had come to differ with Lincoln on the slavery question, and Lincoln now was defending his own point of view. "It is hardly fair for you to assume," he wrote, "that I have no interest in a thing which has, and continually exercises, the power of making me miserable."

As a member of Congress in 1850 Lincoln drafted and introduced a bill for the abolition of slavery in the District of Columbia.

During the 1850's, in his arguments with Stephen A. Douglas, Lincoln spoke often and with eloquence against slavery. On one occasion, in 1854, he said he hated Douglas's attitude of indifference toward the spread of slavery to new areas. "I hate it because of the monstrous injustice of slavery itself," he declared. "I hate it because it deprives our republican example of its just influence in the world — enables the enemies of free institutions, with plausibility, to taunt us as hypocrites." On another occasion Lincoln made his oft-quoted remark that the nation could not long endure half slave and half free. No wonder many Southerners considered him "all broke out" with abolitionism at the time he was elected president.

After he was in the White House, Lincoln continued to express himself eloquently for freedom. In a published reply to Horace Greeley, who was demanding action against slavery, he said (1862) it was his "oft-expressed *personal* wish that all men every where could be free." He confided in a private letter (1864): "I am naturally anti-slavery. If slavery is not wrong, nothing is wrong. I can not remember when I did not so think, and feel." And in a talk to Indiana soldiers (1865) he remarked: "Whenever I hear anyone arguing for slavery I feel a strong impulse to see it tried on him personally."

On the basis of these and other items from the record, Lincoln appears to have been a long-confirmed advocate of freedom, if not an outright abolitionist. But when the whole of the evidence is considered, the conclusion to be drawn is not so clear.

It is not even clear whether in fact Lincoln ever underwent the New Orleans experience which was supposed to have made him an eternal foe of slavery. John Hanks told the anecdote to Herndon in 1865. Hanks had been one of Lincoln's fellow voyagers of the flatboat, but he did not go all the way with the others to New Orleans, so he could not have seen with his own eyes what happened at the slave auction he later described. Herndon said he also heard the story from Lincoln himself. In the account of the journey he gave in his autobiography of 1860, however, Lincoln made no mention of slaves or the slave trade (though of course he intended the autobiography for campaign purposes and could not have been so indiscreet as to emphasize any abolitionist convictions). In the autobiography he also spoke of a previous trip to New Orleans. With regard to this trip, he said nothing about slaves but did refer to Negroes, recalling that he and his one companion "were attacked by seven Negroes with intent to kill and rob them" and were "hurt some in the melee, but succeeded in driving the Negroes from the boat."

As for his stand against the 1837 resolutions of the Illinois legislature, it is enough to point out that he actually took a position against *both sides* of the controversy. Slavery was bad, he held, but he also contended that "the promulgation of abolition doctrines tends rather to increase than to abate its evils."

Regarding the shackled slaves on the Ohio riverboat, he gave at the time an account very different from the one he gave fourteen years afterward to Joshua Speed. Writing to Speed's sister Mary

(September 27, 1841) he described the scene on board the boat quite philosophically as exemplifying "the effect of *condition* upon human happiness." Here were a dozen slaves, "strung together like so many fish upon a trotline," who were being taken from their old Kentucky homes to be sold down the river, who were being separated from families and friends and carried off where slavery was reputed to be at its harshest. Yet, as Lincoln saw them, "they were the most cheerful and apparently happy creatures on board." He concluded that God "renders the worst of human conditions tolerable, while He permits the best, to be nothing better than tolerable."

The point is not that Lincoln was falsifying his emotions when, in the much later account to Speed, he wrote of the sight of those slaves in chains as having been a "continual torment" to him. Certainly he had not forgotten the scene, and very likely he had come to view it in retrospect with heightened feeling. His attitude toward slaves and slavery might well have changed with the passing years — especially the years after 1850, when the issue of slavery extension engrossed national politics.

As late as 1847 his torment apparently was not troublesome enough to deter him from accepting a slaveholder as a law client and arguing against a slave's claim to freedom. Though Illinois presumably was a free state, its laws still provided for Negro servitude of a sort. Under the laws slave labor could be used, provided the slaves were not kept permanently in the state. Slaves worked the Coles County farm of Robert Matson, who brought his blacks from Kentucky every spring and took them back to Kentucky every fall. One of them, Jane Bryant, aroused the ire of Matson's housekeeper and mistress, who demanded that the slave be sold and sent to the Deep South. Jane fled, enlisted the aid of antislavery people, was taken from them, and, lacking the required certificate of freedom, was held in accordance with the Illinois laws. Matson, claiming her as his property, appealed to Lincoln for legal aid. Lincoln took the case and lost.

In Congress, despite his bill for abolition in the District of Columbia, he took a yes-and-no attitude toward slavery. His bill was carefully hedged about so as to offend no slaveholder. It provided for gradual emancipation, with payment to owners, and it was not to go into effect unless approved by the "free white citizens" of the District in a referendum. The bill did not please abolitionists. One of them, Wendell Phillips, called Lincoln "the slave hound of Illinois."

As for his remarks on slavery during the 1850's, it should be borne in mind that Lincoln always was opposing the spread of the institution into the territories. He was not advocating its destruction in the Southern states. When he said the nation could not long remain half slave and half free, but must eventually become all one or the other, he doubtless was thinking of the real danger that the country might become *all slave* — if slavery were allowed to spread. He resisted the aggressive proslavery forces not only because of his concern for the sufferings of blacks, but also because of his concern for the welfare of whites. Again and again he indicated that the civil liberties of every American, white as well as black, were at stake. He insisted upon "keeping the territories free for the settlement of free laborers." He was a Free-Soil man.

"You enquire where I now stand," he wrote in his letter of 1855 to Joshua Speed. "That is a disputed point. I think I am a Whig; but others say there are no Whigs, and that I am an abolitionist." And then he stated the limits of his antislavery zeal as precisely as he could: "I now do no more than oppose the *extension* of slavery." That was where he stood in 1854, and there is no convincing evidence that he had moved beyond that position by 1860 or 1861.

In fact, in the most widely read of his pre-nomination speeches, the one at Cooper Union in New York on February 27, 1860, Lincoln said he agreed with Thomas Jefferson and other founding fathers that slavery should be merely contained, not directly attacked. *"This is all Republicans ask — all Republicans desire — in relation to slavery,"* he emphasized, underlining the words. *"As those fathers marked it, so let it be again marked, as an evil not to be extended, but to be tolerated and protected only because of and so far as its actual presence among us makes that toleration and protection a necessity."* Lincoln further said that emancipation should be most gradual and should be accompanied by deportation of the freed slaves. "In the language of Mr. Jefferson, uttered many years ago, 'It is still in our power to direct the process of emancipation, and deportation, peaceably, and in such slow degrees, as that the evil will wear off insensibly; and their places be, *pari passu,* filled up by free white laborers. If, on the contrary, it is left to force itself on, human nature must shudder at the prospect held up.' "

[2]

As president, even if he personally had desired immediate emancipation, Lincoln had reasons of policy for going slowly with regard to slavery. At the outset of the war the border slave states — Maryland, Delaware, Missouri, and above all Kentucky — hung in the balance. It seemed to Lincoln essential that these states be kept loyal to the Union, and it also seemed to him that a forthright antislavery program might incline them toward the Confederacy.

Whatever the reasons, Lincoln in the beginning was most reluctant to use his presidential powers against slavery. During his first year and more in office he lagged well behind the majority of his party in the cause of freedom. If, as he said, General McClellan had "the slows" when it came to advancing against the Confederate army, he himself had the same affliction when it was a matter of attacking the institution which Alexander H. Stephens called the cornerstone of the Confederacy.

Lincoln held back while Congress and some of his generals went ahead. General John C. Frémont proclaimed freedom for the slaves of disloyal masters in Missouri, and General David Hunter did the same for those in Georgia, South Carolina, and Florida. Lincoln revoked the proclamations of Frémont and Hunter, much to the disgust of all antislavery people, who were growing fast in numbers and in earnestness throughout the North. In the summer of

1861 Congress passed a confiscation act which freed such slaves as the foe put to military use. The next summer Congress passed a second confiscation act, which declared "forever free" all slaves whose owners were in rebellion, whether or not the slaves were being used for military purposes. Lincoln did not veto these laws, but neither did he see that they were faithfully carried out. He considered vetoing the second one, because in his judgment it amounted to an unconstitutional bill of attainder. He did not sign it until it had been amended, and even then he expressed to Congress his dissatisfaction with it.

While hesitating to enforce these laws, Lincoln responded in his own way to the rising sentiment in favor of emancipation. He came forth with a characteristically Lincolnian solution to the slavery problem. His plan contained five elements. First, the states themselves must emancipate the slaves, for in his opinion slavery was a "domestic" institution, the concern of the states alone. Second, slaveowners must be paid for the chattels of which they were to be deprived. Third, the federal government must share the financial burden by providing federal bonds as grants-in-aid to the states. Fourth, the actual freeing of the slaves must not be hurried; the states must be given plenty of time, delaying final freedom until as late as 1900 if they wished. Fifth, the freed Negroes must be shipped out of the country and colonized abroad, but they must be persuaded to go willingly. State action, compensation, federal aid, gradual emancipation, and voluntary colonization — these were the indispensable features of the Lincoln plan.

To carry out this plan he had to gain the approval of Congress, the border slave states, and the leaders of the Negro race. Congress responded affirmatively but without enthusiasm, indicating its willingness to vote the necessary funds. None of the border politicians were won over to the scheme, however, and very few Negroes could be persuaded to leave their native land, the United States.

Three times in the spring of 1862 Lincoln appealed to the border-state congressmen. He told them that, if their states would only act, the war soon would be over; for the Confederacy lived upon the hope of winning the border states, and, once these had declared for freedom, that hope would be gone. He warned the congressmen that, if their states refused to act, slavery in time would disappear anyhow. It would be destroyed "by mere friction and abrasion — by the mere incidents of war." The border states, he eloquently said, had before them the grand opportunity of saving the Union. But he made no headway whatsoever; again and again they rejected the opportunity.

Meanwhile, he did not let up in his efforts to talk the free Negroes into leaving the country. Some of their own leaders advocated starting life anew in the Negro republic of Liberia or Haiti. Lincoln preferred Central America as their new home. In his eagerness he was taken in by a group of land speculators who offered to sell the Chiriqui territory on the isthmus of Panama. They pictured Chiriqui as a land rich in coal, among other things, but eventually became so effusive in their praises of this tropical paradise it became clear that their title was dubious and the resources nonexistent.

He was nevertheless loath to give up the colonization idea itself. He invited to the White House a group of five prominent Negroes — the first of their race a president ever so honored — and he honored them further by saying frankly that there was no place for them and their people in the United States. Though they might be treated better in the North than in the South, they would suffer discrimination everywhere so long as they remained in this country. "The ban," he said, "is still upon you." From Negroes who heard of this interview, the response was most unfavorable. One wrote to Lincoln: "Pray tell us is our right to a home in this country less than your own?"

If, in the summer of 1862, Lincoln had had his way, the later history of this country would have been radically changed. For instance, if the states had adopted his plan, there would probably be few Negroes left in the country, North or South. By 1900 the slaves of the border states would have been set free and sent abroad. The slaves of the Confederate states, if these states too had chosen to adopt the Lincoln plan, would have enjoyed the same fortune or suffered the same fate.

If, on the other hand, the war had come to an early end, as Lincoln hoped, the slaves of the Confederate states could have been left in bondage indefinitely, or at least until they were freed by some hand other than his. Even in the border states, after emancipation, slavery might have been reestablished by state action. What these states had done, they could undo, according to Lincoln's conception of state's rights. Indeed, in order to discourage this contingency, he drafted an emancipation bill containing the proviso that, if any state should abolish and then reintroduce the institution, it would have to return to the federal government the federal funds it had received as a grant-in-aid!

[3]

President Lincoln did not behave like a great emancipator during his first year-and-a-half in office. The question is, did he change his mind and his policy after that? More particularly, did he intend — with the preliminary proclamation of September 21, 1862, and the final one of January 1, 1863 — to free the slaves?

According to most accounts, he did. Despite his campaign pledges and the constraints of the Constitution, argue supporters of this position, he decided that he must strike at slavery for reasons of military necessity. He came to this conclusion, and drafted a fitting proclamation, in July 1862. When he read this draft to his cabinet, Seward advised him to withhold the announcement until the Union armies had won a victory on the battlefield. Otherwise, Seward cautioned, the proclamation might sound like a confession of military failure, like "the last *shriek* on our retreat." So Lincoln stalled, awaiting the hoped-for victory. When a delegation of Chicago churchmen appealed to him, he asked them whether a proclamation would do any good, whether it would not be as futile as the pope's legendary bull against the comet. Before they left, he assured them that he had not decided against a proclamation but held the matter under advisement. When Horace Greeley in the *New York Tribune* called upon him to make freedom a reality, he patiently replied (August 22, 1862): "My paramount object in this struggle *is* to save the Union, and is *not* either to save or to destroy slavery. If I could save the Union without freeing *any* slave I would do it, and if I could save it by freeing *all* the slaves I would do it; and if I could do it by freeing some and leaving others alone I would also do that." At last McClellan's checking of Lee at Antietam gave Lincoln at least a substitute for victory, and a few days later he accordingly issued the document he had long since decided upon.

This is a familiar story, and there is a certain amount of evidence to give it historical substance. There is, for example, the record Welles made of a conversation Lincoln had with him and Seward on Sunday, July 13, while on a carriage ride to a funeral. "It was on this occasion and on this ride that he first mentioned to Mr. Seward and myself the subject of emancipating the slaves by proclamation in case the Rebels did not cease to persist in their war on the Government and the Union, of which he saw no evidence," Welles wrote afterward. "He dwelt earnestly on the gravity, importance, and delicacy of the movement, said he had given it much thought and had about come to the conclusion that it was a military necessity absolutely essential for the salvation of the Union, that we must free the slaves or be ourselves subdued, etc., etc." Welles added this comment: "It was a new departure for the President, for until this time, in all our previous interviews, whenever the question of emancipation or the mitigation of slavery had been in any way alluded to, he had been prompt and emphatic in denouncing any interference by the General Government with the subject."

Welles may have remembered accurately what the president said on that Sunday, though the record of the conversation is not a regular diary entry but a reminiscence that the diarist put down after the lapse of considerable time. And Lincoln, if Welles summarized his sentiments accurately, may have meant what he said. Yet in the ensuing weeks others who saw Lincoln reported him as saying things that seemed to belie his determination to proclaim freedom for the slaves. When Greeley visited the White House to repeat the plea of his *Tribune* editorial, Lincoln protested that he dared not antagonize Kentuckians and impel them to desert to the rebel side. He expressed this same concern to others, including the Chicago religious group. If he really had made his decision and was only waiting for the auspicious moment to proclaim it, he might have put off his tormenters by frankly telling them so. As it was, he left even some of his official advisers to wonder whether he would ever issue the proclamation he had read to the cabinet.

These inconsistencies of his have led to the suspicion that, until after the battle of Antietam, he made no irrevocable commitment even to himself. Here and there he dropped hints that he might issue the proclamation — and then again might not. Apparently his purpose was to prepare his hearers for the possibility that he might call the whole thing off. He was waiting for a decisive victory, but if that kind of victory had come, he might have forgotten about the proclamation. Some historians claim that he dusted it off and give it to the world only when he learned the true proportions of Antietam. McClellan, though he turned Lee back, had let him get away. If McClellan had administered a crushing defeat, the proclamation might have stayed in its pigeonhole.

This theory depends on the supposition that Lincoln at the time was concerned not so much about military necessity as about political necessity. He had to contend with a strong bloc of Republicans in Congress, headed by Thaddeus Stevens in the House and Charles Sumner and Henry Wilson in the Senate, backed by a majority of the party, who had become Radicals on the slave question. They were demanding that the President carry out the laws, the confiscation acts, the act for the enrollment of Negro troops. They held the firm conviction that, to win the war, the government must free the slaves and use them against their former masters. As their strongest argument, the Radicals cited the succession

27

of Union defeats on the Virginia front. The way the war was being fought, it was not being won, and it therefore must be fought another way. There was even the possibility that they might try to stop the flow of money and supplies if Lincoln did not give in. Only a conclusive victory, only a dramatic refutation of the Radical argument would restore his freedom of action. He prayed for such a victory, and then came the disappointing news of Antietam.

To pursue this argument to its logical conclusion, Lincoln then pulled out the proclamation as his trump. In issuing it he did not really yield to the Radicals. Rather, he outfoxed them. At first they hailed the document as a triumph for them and their cause, but soon they were disillusioned, since the proclamation had as its purpose and effect the checking of the Radical program. Having announced in September that he would make a final proclamation the first of the following year, Lincoln had an excuse for disregarding the laws about confiscation and Negro troops throughout the intervening months. He also had a policy with which to frustrate Stevens's drive for legislation to make soldiers and freemen out of slaves from the border states. During the months of delay he hoped at last to gain approval for his own plan, the familiar plan of gradual emancipation by the states themselves, with federal funds to pay to slaveowners and to rid the country of the freed slaves.

There is testimony from some of the men who knew Lincoln to give credence to this view. There is, for instance, the testimony of Edward Stanly, a proslavery, state's-rights, Unionist North Carolinian whom Lincoln had appointed as military governor of the occupied North Carolina coast. Stanly had taken the job with the understanding that Lincoln would not interfere with slavery in the states. Once the proclamation had been issued, Stanly went to Washington intending to resign. After several talks with Lincoln, however, Stanly was satisfied. He returned to his job, but first he called at the office of James C. Welling, editor of the *National Intelligencer.* Welling wrote in his diary: "Mr. Stanly said that the President had stated to him that the proclamation had become a civil necessity to prevent the Radicals from openly embarrassing the government in the conduct of the war."

Quite apart from testimony such as this, a fairly strong inference of Lincoln's delaying tactics can be drawn from the text of the proclamation. The preliminary announcement said that after January 1, 1863, the slaves in states then still in rebellion would be considered free. The final proclamation excluded from the area of freedom not only the loyal border states but all the Confederate states and parts of states that the Union forces had occupied. As cynics pointed out at the time, Lincoln was leaving the slaves untouched in places where he had the ability to free them, and he was offering liberty only to those he had no power to reach. Congress already had enabled him to do more than this. The second confiscation act provided for the liberation of all slaves belonging to disloyal masters, regardless of the masters' residence. Instead of issuing the kind of proclamation that he did, Lincoln needed only to proclaim that he was enforcing the second confiscation act, and then he could have proceeded to order the seizure of enemy-owned slaves in every place where the Union armies got control — if his object truly had been to weaken the enemy by making inroads into his Negro manpower.

Lincoln himself gave indisputable proof that, after the preliminary proclamation, he remained as passionately devoted as ever to his own gradual emancipation scheme. In his message to Congress of December 1, 1862, just one month before the final proclamation, he had little to say about that forthcoming pronouncement and much to say about his favored plan. He proposed a constitutional amendment to put the plan into effect. On this subject he reached one of the peaks of his eloquence. "Fellow-citizens, *we* cannot escape history," he said. "We of this Congress and this administration, will be remembered in spite of ourselves. The fiery trial through which we pass, will light us down, in honor or dishonor, to the latest generation." These words are justly famous. What is often forgotten is the fact that they were conceived as part of a plea for deporting American-born Negroes from

America. Lincoln in this message actually used the word *deportation,* as if he had in the back of his mind the thought of resorting, if necessary, to the compulsion which that word implies.

No inspired phrases were to be found in the paper that Lincoln signed with the gold pen, in the quavering hand, on January 1, 1863. In itself this proclamation was a dull and prosaic document — no ringing call to freedom. The proclamation had some effect in attracting slaves out of rebeldom and into the Union lines, where they were set free, but the existing laws of Congress provided for that much and more. After two years, when the war was ending, Lincoln estimated that some 200,000 slaves had gained their liberty under his edict. That was only about one in twenty of the total number of slaves, and even that minority had no sure hold on freedom. Lincoln himself doubted the constitutionality of his step, except as a temporary war measure. After the war the freedmen would have risked reenslavement, had nothing else been done to confirm their liberty.

All this does not necessarily disprove the commonly accepted story of what Lincoln did or tried to do in signing his famous proclamation. Maybe he meant to hasten freedom, maybe to delay it. Nobody knows.

[4]

Actual freedom for the Negroes — or at least the end of chattel slavery — came in consequence of the Thirteenth Amendment. President Lincoln played a part in bringing about this constitutional change, yet he was slow to take an out-and-out antislavery stand; indeed, he gave some indications that his conversion never was complete.

He did not claim to have originated the idea of such an amendment, though the abolitionists did. At Cleveland in May 1864, a group of these extreme Republicans nominated John C. Frémont for the ·presidency and adopted a platform with a Thirteenth Amendment as the key plank.

When the regular Republicans met in convention the following month, Lincoln was aware of the need for winning the dissidents back to the party fold. He called to the White House the chairman of the Republican National Committee, Senator E. D. Morgan, and gave him instructions for his speech opening the convention. "Senator Morgan," he is reported to have said, "I want you to mention in your speech when you call the convention to order, as its keynote, and to put into the platform as the keystone, the amendment of the Constitution abolishing and prohibiting slavery forever." Senator Morgan did as the president wished. That platform included a plank stating that slavery was the cause of the rebellion, that the president's proclamations had aimed "a death blow at this gigantic evil," and that a a constitutional amendment was necessary to "terminate and forever prohibit" it. Undoubtedly the delegates would have adopted such a plank whether or not Lincoln, through Senator Morgan, had urged it.

When Lincoln was reelected on this platform and the Republican majority in Congress was increased, he was justified in feeling, as he apparently did, that he had a popular mandate for the Thirteenth Amendment. The newly chosen Congress, with its overwhelming Republican majority, would not meet until after the lame duck session of the old Congress during the winter of 1864-65. But Lincoln did not wait. Using all his resources of patronage and persuasion on certain of the Democrats, he managed to get the necessary two-thirds vote before the session's end. He rejoiced as the amendment went out to the states for ratification, and he rejoiced again and again as his own Illinois led off and other states followed one by one in acting favorably upon it. He did not live to rejoice in its ultimate adoption.

Yet, for all he did to see that freedom finally was written into the fundamental law, Lincoln to the last seemed to have a lingering preference for another kind of amendment, another kind of plan. He still clung to his old ideas of postponing final emancipation, compensating slaveholders, and colonizing freedmen. Or so it would appear. As late as March 1865, if the somewhat question-

31

able Ben Butler is to be believed, Lincoln summoned him to the White House to discuss the feasibility of removing the colored population of the United States.

[5]

Lincoln is a paradoxical hero. His name has been lighted down from generation to generation as a synonym for liberty and equality. His name also has been made to symbolize the opposite doctrine of white supremacy and black oppression.

Lincoln the friend of freedom is well and widely known. For most liberals he occupies a place beside Thomas Jefferson. For many Negroes he long has held a lone position as a kind of folk god.

His exaltation dates back to January 1, 1863, when throughout the North and the conquered areas of the South the colored people held proclamation meetings to celebrate his deed in their behalf. At a Washington meeting which began on New Year's Eve, a pastor told each member of his flock to "get down on *both knees* to thank Almighty God for his freedom and President Lincoln too." To people such as these the proclamation, whatever its inward meaning, was the outward sign of an answer to their prayers.

Most of the abolitionists joined in honoring Lincoln at the time of his emancipation edict, but some of them qualified their praise, still doubting his sincerity. At last, when he had won congressional approval for the Thirteenth Amendment, almost all the lingering doubts were dispelled and almost all the doubters satisfied. Even William Lloyd Garrison no longer could contain himself. To a Boston meeting of celebrators Garrison said: "And to whom is the country more immediately indebted for this vital and saving amendment of the Constitution than, perhaps, to any other man? I believe I may confidently answer — to the humble rail splitter of Illinois — to the Presidential chainbreaker for millions of the oppressed — to Abraham Lincoln!"

Less well known than Lincoln the slaves' chainbreaker is Lincoln the hero of Negro-baiters and white supremacists. Yet his has been that kind of image also. Few Negroes or friends of the Negro ever admired him more or praised him oftener than did a certain Mississippi advocate of white supremacy, James K. Vardaman. In the early 1900's this long-haired, dramatic great white chief of Mississippi stood out as the most rabid racialist in the most racist-dominated Southern state. When Theodore Roosevelt dined with the Negro educator Booker T. Washington in the White House, Vardaman sneered at the president as a "wild broncho buster and coon-flavored miscegenationist." In his campaign for the gover-norship Vardaman said that if he were in office he would do what he could to protect a captured Negro "fiend" from a lynching mob. "But if I were a private citizen I would head the mob to string the brute up, and I haven't much respect for a white man who wouldn't." As governor, he opposed what he called "this policy of spoiling young Negroes by educating them." In the Senate dur-ing World War I he took every opportunity to expound his belief in a white man's country. Do not draft Negroes into the army, he advised his fellow senators, for it is dangerous to give them a sense of citizenship and a training in the use of guns. Repeal the Fif-teenth Amendment so that Negroes cannot even pretend to have the right to vote. Enforce segregation and do not let the races mix, for the Negro is by nature morally inferior and must never be al-lowed to corrupt the pure blood of the heaven-favored white. Such were the aims and convictions to which Vardaman devoted his real eloquence.

This Mississippian once made a pilgrimage to his hero's home town, Springfield, Illinois. The year was 1909, the centennial of Lincoln's birth. The previous year had been a disgraceful one for Springfield. Municipal leaders were looking ahead to anniversary celebrations when, on a summer night, thousands of the towns-people suddenly went wild with hate. They set out to lynch a Ne-gro who (though innocent) was being held on the charge of raping a white woman; when the sheriff frustrated them by spiriting the man away, they turned their vengeance upon the whole colored

33

community. It took four thousand state troopers all of a week to quiet the city and end the so-called race riot. (This incident, by the way, and not some crisis in the South, gave rise to the National Association for the Advancement of Colored People.) When Vardaman visited Springfield, the feeling among local negrophobes still ran high, and a huge crowd came out to applaud his lecture on the inherent virtue of the white race.

Vardaman never tired of praising "the immortal Lincoln," never tired of quoting "the wise words of this wondrous man." He insisted that he and Lincoln saw eye to eye. "I have made a very careful study of Mr. Lincoln's ideas on this question," he declared in a Senate speech, "and I have said often, and I repeat here, that my views and his on the race question are substantially identical." Next to Thomas Jefferson, he thought, Lincoln understood the Negro problem better than anyone else of former days. To prove his point, Vardaman cited Lincoln's advocacy of Negro colonization. He explained the Lincoln policy thus:

> Up to the very time of Mr. Lincoln's death he told the Negroes who came to see him here in Washington, "You will not be permitted to share in the government of this country, and I am not prepared to say that you ought to be, if I had the power to give you that right."
>
> He said further: "The shackles of slavery will be stricken from your arms. You, the educated and more fortunate members of your race, take the others and go to some country" — his idea was the same that Jefferson's was — "and there work out your own salvation." I do not pretend to quote Mr. Lincoln literally. The great desire of his patriotic heart was that the friction might be avoided by deportation.

The words of Lincoln that Vardaman repeated oftenest, the words he knew almost by heart, came from the debate with Douglas at Charleston, Illinois, on September 18, 1858. These words formed for Vardaman a sort of golden text. Here they are, exactly as Lincoln uttered them:

> I will say then that I am not, nor ever have been in favor of bring-

ing about in any way the social and political equality of the white and black races, [applause] — that I am not nor ever have been in favor of making voters or jurors of Negroes, nor of qualifying them to hold office, nor to intermarry with white people; and I will say in addition to this that there is a physical difference between the white and black races which I believe will forever forbid the two races living together on terms of social and political equality. And inasmuch as they cannot so live, while they do remain together there must be the position of superior and inferior, and I as much as any other man am in favor of having the superior position assigned to the white race.

[6]

Yet, despite these contradictions, Lincoln does deserve his reputation as emancipator. True, his claim to the honor is supported very uncertainly, if at all, by the proclamation itself. The honor has a better basis in the support he gave to the Thirteenth Amendment. It is well founded also in his greatness as the war leader who carried the nation safely through the four-year struggle that brought freedom in its train. But the best reason for his reputation is, perhaps, to be discovered in something else. Consider the example he set his fellow Americans by treating all men as human beings, regardless of the pigment of their skin.

The real and final emancipation of the Negro may depend more upon attitudes than upon laws. The laws, the constitutional amendments, are important, even indispensable. But, as the abolitionist Henry Wilson observed, many of those who voted for the Thirteenth Amendment and other antislavery measures did so without conversion or conviction. Many acted from a desire to hurt the slaveholder rather than to help the slave. Within their hearts still lurked the "foul spirit of caste," the spirit of race prejudice. Until this prejudice was overcome, the Negroes, though no longer the slaves of individual masters, would continue to be in a sense the slaves of the community as a whole.

Now, Lincoln himself was one of those who veered to an actively antislavery line for reasons of wartime expediency. He did not pretend to do otherwise. And he was well aware of race prejudice as an existing fact in the United States; hence, his pathetic eagerness to find new homes for freedmen in foreign lands. Yet he had the capacity to rise above prejudice, and he grandly rose above it. Again and again, during the last two years of his life, he made the White House a scene of practical demonstrations of respect for human worth and dignity. He proved that whites and Negroes, without the master-servant tie, could get along together happily in his own official home, no matter what the antagonisms that might trouble the nation at large. A kindly, unself-conscious host, he greeted Negro visitors as no president had done before.

The distinguished former slave Frederick Douglass called upon Lincoln several times at his summer cottage at the Soldiers' Home. Douglass made at least three visits to the White House. On the final occasion, when he tried to enter as an invited guest at the inaugural reception in 1865, policemen manhandled him and forced him out. Making his way in again, he managed to catch Lincoln's eye. "Here comes my friend Douglass," the president exclaimed, and, leaving the circle of guests he had been conversing with, he took Douglass by the hand and began to chat with him. Years later Douglass wrote: "In all my interviews with Mr. Lincoln I was impressed with his entire freedom from popular prejudice against the colored race. He was the first great man that I talked with in the United States freely, who in no single instance reminded me of the difference between himself and myself, of the difference of color, and I thought that all the more remarkable because he came from a state where there were black laws."

There were black laws in Illinois indeed — laws that denied the Negro the vote and deprived him of other rights. Illinois in those days was a Jim Crow state. That was where Lincoln had spent most of the years of his manhood, among people who had migrated from slave country farther south, as he himself had done. Naturally he had shared some of the negrophobic feeling of his neighbors in Kentucky, in southern Indiana, in central Illinois. That was where, in geography and in sentiment, he came from.

But he did not stay there. The most remarkable thing about him was his tremendous power of growth. He grew in sympathy, in the breadth of his humaneness, as he grew in other aspects of the mind and spirit. In more ways than one he succeeded in breaking through the narrow bounds of his early environment.

This helps to explain and to reconcile those conflicting images of Lincoln — on the one hand, the racist; on the other, the champion of the common man, black as well as white. The one view reflects the position he started from, the other the position he was moving toward. There is confusion regarding particular phases of his presidential career because nobody knows for sure just what point he had reached at any given moment. But there should be little question as to which way he was going.

To see Lincoln in this light is to make him more than ever relevant, more than ever inspiring, for us in the stormy present, in the fiery trial through which we too must pass. Lincoln, as a symbol of man's ability to outgrow his prejudices, still serves the cause of human freedom. He will go on serving so long as boundaries of color hem in and hinder any man, any woman, any child.

NOTES

1. All the biographers, of course, treat with comparative fullness the subject of Lincoln and slavery. A basic work, by a wartime Illinois congressman who knew the president and who stressed the antislavery theme in his career, is Isaac N. Arnold's *The History of Abraham Lincoln and the Overthrow of American Slavery* (Chicago: Clarke, 1866). A later work by Arnold, again emphasizing this theme, is *The Life of Abraham Lincoln* (Chicago: Jansen, McClurg, 1885). Another useful work by a contemporary antislavery politician is Henry Wilson's *History of the Rise and Fall of the Slave Power in America* (Boston: Houghton Mifflin; Osgood, 1872-77). Probably the best exposition of Lincoln's own preferred emancipation plan is to be found in the second volume of J. G. Randall's *Lincoln the President* (New York: Dodd, Mead, 1945-55).

A recent and forthright statement of the view that Lincoln used his famous proclamation as a dodge to delay actual freedom is presented by

Ralph Korngold in *Thaddeus Stevens: A Being Darkly Wise and Rudely Great* (New York: Harcourt, Brace, 1955), especially ch. 7, "The Truth about the Emancipation Proclamation." Some contemporary impressions of Lincoln's slow and incomplete conversion to the antislavery cause are recorded in Allen T. Rice, ed., *Reminiscences of Abraham Lincoln* (New York: North American, 1885). On Lincoln's relationships with Negroes, see Frederick Douglass's recollections in the Rice volume; Benjamin Quarles, *The Negro in the Civil War* (Boston: Little, Brown, 1953); and Warren A. Beck, "Lincoln and Negro Colonization in Central America," *Abraham Lincoln Quarterly* (1950).

James K. Vardaman's views on Lincoln and the Negro are repeated and elaborated in a number of his Senate speeches, two of which have been noted in particular, those of February 6, 1914, and August 16, 1917, in the *Congressional Record*. There is a sketch of Vardaman in the *Dictionary of American Biography*, and there are several contemporary magazine articles concerning him. No full-length study of the man had been published when "The Friend of Freedom" was written. Since then, two biographies have appeared: William F. Holmes, *The White Chief: James Kimble Vardaman* (Baton Rouge: Louisiana State University Press, 1970), and George C. Osborne, *James Kimble Vardaman, Southern Commoner* (Jackson, Miss.: Hederman Bros., 1981).

⟦ III ⟧

The Lincoln Theme —
Unexhausted and Inexhaustible

IT IS FITTING that we should pause to take stock of recent Lincoln scholarship, now that the sesquicentennial is closing and, incidentally, now that a second century of Lincoln studies is beginning. A hundred years ago, in June, appeared the first of the campaign biographies, the first book about Lincoln, the first raindrop in what was eventually to become a torrent of publications. It would be much too much to undertake, at the moment, even the most general appraisal of that whole century of writing. It is rash enough to attempt a review of the last quarter-century alone. This review must be brief. Only the most significant new findings can be noticed, and those but cursorily. A great deal of very valuable work must go unmentioned.

Fortunately we have a kind of benchmark against which to measure the progress of the past twenty-five years. The *American Historical Review* for January 1936 included an essay by that prince of Lincoln scholars and finest of men, James G. Randall. The title of Randall's essay is familiar — so familiar to historians that among

Address at a symposium on "The Current State of Lincoln Scholarship," Library of Congress, Washington, D.C., February 11, 1960. Reprinted from *Abraham Lincoln Sesquicentennial, 1959-1960: Final Report of the Lincoln Sesquicentennial Commission* (Washington: Government Printing Office, 1960), pp. 175-82.

them it has often been the subject of parody and jest (which, it must be said, the author himself had the sense of humor to enjoy). The title: "Has the Lincoln Theme Been Exhausted?" In the essay Randall noted the vast quantity of books, brochures, speeches, and miscellaneous effusions already in print and dryly called attention to the variety of topics, among them a number such as this: "Dogs Were Ever a Joy to Lincoln." He remarked upon the "spurious nature of much that passes for Lincoln scholarship," and he observed that "among comprehensive biographers who have made Lincoln their main interest the trained historical specialist is rarely seen." His basic argument he summarized in these words:

> The general reader, vaguely aware of the multitude of Lincoln writings, or the historian who has specialized elsewhere, might suppose that the Lincoln theme had been sufficiently developed. If, however, one finds that in the sources there is both spadework and refining work to be done, that the main body of Lincoln manuscripts is closed to research, that no definitive edition of the works is to be had, that genuine Lincoln documents are continually coming to light while false ones receive unmerited credence, and that collateral studies bearing upon Lincoln are being steadily developed, then any conclusion as to the exhaustion of the theme would appear premature. If the investigator further discovers that there are obscure points to be searched, disputed points to be pondered, lacunae to be filled, revisionist interpretations to be applied or tested, excellent studies yet to be published, others in progress, valuable projects still to be undertaken, and finally, that an adequate, full-length biography (comparable, let us say, to Freeman's new life of Lee) is still in the future, then he realizes that, far from being exhausted, the field is rich in opportunity.

When we reread this statement of Randall's — and the list of particulars with which he accompanied it — we cannot help being amazed at the contrast between the achievements and opportunities in Lincoln scholarship today and the achievements and opportunities of one short generation ago. We now have, of course, Carl Sandburg's magnificent four volumes on *The War Years*. We have Randall's own four volumes presenting *Lincoln the President* with unmatched thoughtfulness and objectivity and applying rigorously the "revisionist intepretations" that he had called for. In the Library of Congress we have access to the manuscript treasures of the Herndon-Weik and, far more important, the Robert Todd Lincoln collection, which we are inclined to use without sufficient appreciation, forgetting how recently they were made available. We now possess that "definitive edition of the works" which, when Randall wrote his famous essay, was still nearly twenty years in the future. And at last we have trustworthy editions of those invaluable cabinet diaries that refract the president's image through the very different personalities of Salmon P. Chase and Gideon Welles.[1] Of the specific studies that Randall listed in 1936 as needing to be done, a large number have since appeared in print, among them the following: "an examination of the letters and papers of Lincoln's biographers,"[2] "a truly adequate study of Lincoln as president-elect," and monographs on such collateral subjects as William H. Herndon and the war governors. Numerous other phases of the Lincoln theme have been treated in studies that Randall did not happen to foresee.

In the light of all this work we must revise our conception of Lincoln at various points in his career. At each of these points we are presented a much more accurate and sharply focused picture, if in some respects a less colorful one, than could be had as recently as 1936. We must clear from our minds the false or dubious conceptions that formerly prevailed.

No longer, for example, can we imagine the seven-year-old Abraham as spending his first Indiana winter in a "half-faced camp," a kind of lean-to with one side open and protected only by a blazing fire. Very likely his father built such a shelter when marking off the land in advance of the family's arrival, but there is no reason to believe that Abraham and his mother and sister actually lived in this crude structure, except possibly for a few days while a regular cabin was being put up. Thomas Lincoln, by no means the ne'er-do-well he used to be considered, doubtless erected that first cabin in a hurry, with the customary aid of his neighbors. If we must abandon the notion that Thomas was a shiftless man, we must also give up the pleasant fiction that his wife Nancy was a woman of unusual talents, a woman at whose knee Abraham learned his letters by firelight. Indeed, on the whole matter of his early education and his youthful book borrowing and reading habits, we must be guided by a strong and steady skepticism.

No longer can we think of Lincoln the lawyer as a person of such excessive and unrealistic scruple that he seldom took criminal cases and never did so unless he was assured of his client's innocence. As a very recent authority rather belligerently puts the matter: "Lincoln's showing in the Truett trial, as in numerous other of his cases, where the facts were overwhelmingly against his client, should dispose, with devastating finality, of the patent poppycock advanced by certain of his biographers — even by some of his contemporaries — that Lincoln could only put forth his best efforts when convinced of the justice of the cause which he advocated." It seems that Lincoln, like any capable and conscientious attorney, gave his clients full value for their fees, regardless of what he thought of the justice of their case. And he *was* a capable and conscientious attorney, one of the very best in Illinois.[3]

Yet afterward his longtime partner William H. Herndon made many "piddling references" to his legal abilities and showed practically no awareness of his real achievements at the bar. Thus we can no longer put much faith in Herndon even when he is dealing with matters presumably within his personal knowledge. He cannot be trusted on the subject he ought to have known the most about — Lincoln and the law. And certainly, as has been realized for some time, he cannot be trusted on things he had no personal knowledge of, such as Lincoln's supposed love affairs and his home life. The Herndon view of Ann Rutledge and of Mary Todd has been deprived, within the last several years, of what little credibility it still had left.[4] At last we can see that the issue between the Herndon school of biography and its critics was not one of realism versus romanticism, for Herndon himself was a special kind of romantic, and he often had little regard for factual reality.[5]

No longer can we consider Lincoln as a man lacking in money sense, a man so impecunious that, as it has been said, he had to borrow the railroad fare from Springfield to Washington before he could make the trip for his inauguration. Meticulous research has shown that he was worth at least $15,000 at the time of his election, that he saved more than half of his presidential salary, and that at his death he left an estate afterward appraised at $83,000.

These are some of the corrections that must be made in our knowledge of Lincoln's personal life. When we turn to his public career, we find still more important changes to be made in our thinking. His presidential years, obviously the most significant, have been until recently the most neglected. It used to be that his greatness in statesmanship was taken pretty much for granted. At last we have been given information and ideas adding sharpness to our vision, letting us come closer than before to beholding the true elements of his greatness.

Since 1936, Lincoln the politician has been the subject of several informative and revealing books. *Congressman Abraham Lincoln,* a critical account which corrects the classic volumes of Albert J. Beveridge at several points, shows the lone Whig from Illinois busily "politicking" throughout his one term in the House of Representatives.[6] His later growth in political skill stands out sharply against the ineptitude he often displayed during that congressional term. Much of his progress in the art of politics is to be seen in *Lincoln's Rise to Power,* a realistic study of his nomination in 1860, which points the moral that, if we seek the man who made Lincoln president, we should look into the activities of Lincoln himself.[7]

Even after his election, as we see in *Lincoln and the War Governors,* he remained at first something of a creature of the separate state Republican organizations. By the time of his reelection in 1864, he had advanced a long way toward the formation of a unified national or at least all-Northern party, with himself at its head.[8]

One of the chief sources of his strength, we learn in *Lincoln and the Patronage,* lay in his control of government jobs. From day to day, down to the very last day of his life, he kept at his often disagreeable patronage chores, deciding upon a federal marshal here, a postmaster there. This was a grubby business but a necessary one.[9] His devotion to it strengthens the view, presented in *Lincoln Reconsidered,* that he depended less than other strong presidents upon direct appeals to Congress or the people. He worked mostly behind the scenes, with other organization men of his party. He was, in short, a "politician's politician."[10] We do not think any the less of him for all this. "In being a competent politician," the students of his use of patronage point out, "he became a statesman."

In a thoughtful essay on *The Statesmanship of the Civil War* we are informed that Lincoln possessed in high degree the five qualities that go to make up a statesman: intellectual power, moral strength, a feeling for the spirit and needs of the time, an instinctive understanding of the masses, and some kind of passion — in his case, a passion for democracy. Most of the countless new books and articles dealing with Civil War subjects involve the wartime president, closely or remotely, and they throw varying amounts of light upon his qualities of statecraft. Indeed, the more thoroughly the war as a whole is investigated, the more conspicuously he stands out as the great "hero of the conflict." The author of *The Ordeal of the Union,* that projected ten-volume work reanalyzing the whole period of division and reunion, concludes at midpoint in the study: "Well it was for the Republic that out of such a political milieu rose a Chief Executive who combined the noblest qualities of the heart with a singularly lucid intellect and a piercing vision."[11]

Lincoln, of course, was a military as well as a civil leader, and his role as commander-in-chief has come to be much better appreciated than ever before. For many years after his death the balance of expert opinion leaned to the view that he had been an ignoramus in military matters and that he commanded best when he commanded least. All along, however, there were those who held that he had directed the war with real competence, and a few arose to proclaim that he had been no less than a military genius. Still even his warmest admirers assumed that, early in 1864, he had ceased to exercise his talent actively, that he had turned the whole responsibility over to Ulysses S. Grant upon the latter's elevation to supreme command. Recently, in the book *Lincoln and His Generals,* a much more thoroughgoing thesis has been cogently argued: namely, that Lincoln remained the guiding spirit of the Union armies to the very end of the war.[12] Though the subject is susceptible of differences in interpretation and emphasis, there can now be little doubt that one of his most important contributions lay in the field of grand strategy.

Lincoln made another contribution that, until a few years ago, was scarcely guessed at. During the war he served as a kind of informal, one-man office of scientific research and development. Inventors and promoters brought him their proposals for new arms and ammunition. He put the more promising ideas to a practical test, sometimes firing an experimental gun himself, in a weedy lot between the White House and the Washington Monument. If an invention seemed worth using, he urged it upon the Ordnance Bureau or, in some cases, upon the generals in the field. Thus he aided signally in the development and adoption of mortars, explosive bullets, incendiary shells, repeating rifles, and even machine guns. The story is told in *Lincoln and the Tools of War,* a book written by a scholar who, combining the talents of a historian and an engineer, discovered and made use of Ordnance Bureau records that had lain almost untouched.[13] This work is an excellent example of the kind of research opportunity that was unforeseen in 1936 and that, indeed, is always unforeseen until someone happens to get a bright idea.

For all the new information and new insights that have been brought into view, and for all the myths and falsehoods that have been brushed aside, there still remain phases of the Lincoln story with regard to which we have only a rather clouded and fuzzy picture. There still remain unsolved puzzles, unsettled controversies.

For instance, is the "Diary of a Public Man" reliable, and who was its author? That diary, published anonymously in the *North American Review* in 1879, contains interesting sidelights on Lincoln — interesting if true.[14] Again, was Lincoln wholly right, and McClellan wholly wrong, in their disagreements over the peninsula campaign? The answer has a bearing on our judgment of Lincoln as a war leader, for if McClellan was a comparatively good general, then Lincoln was a correspondingly poor commander-in-chief, at least in 1862.

Did Lincoln, in 1864, choose Andrew Johnson as his running mate and use quiet influence to bring about Johnson's nomination? This is a tricky kind of problem in historical detection, for Lincoln had to be secretive if he actually did what he is said to have done, and so he would have left no good documentary tracks for the historian to follow.[15] Was Lincoln, as William T. Sherman afterward said, the real author of the peace terms that Sherman offered to Joseph E. Johnston? By the time the Sherman-Johnston convention was signed, Lincoln was dead. His views must be inferred from bits and pieces of conflicting evidence.

While there are as yet no generally agreed-upon answers to questions such as the foregoing, the search for answers has by no means been wasted effort. At the very least, issues have been sharpened and clarified, facts have been established, fictions disposed of, and the whole discussion has been elevated to a more sophisticated plane than heretofore. We may look forward to eventual arrival at a consensus or a near-consensus on most of the disputes.

There are, however, some controversies about Lincoln that may never be put completely to rest. Some controversies are rooted largely in emotion, not entirely in reason, and hence are not quite amenable to objective fact or impartial thought. The outstanding example is the question of Lincoln and Fort Sumter.

No sooner had Sumter fallen than enemies of Lincoln, especially Confederate leaders, began to charge that he had deliberately maneuvered the Confederates into firing the first shot and thus had brought on a needless war. Not until 1937 was this charge elaborated, documented, and published in a scholarly work. Since then, both the attack and the defense have been carried to extremes. On the one side, it has been asserted that Lincoln even faked the need for supplies at Sumter so as to have an excuse for provisioning the fort and thus provoking a fight. On the other side, it has been maintained that he planned and expected a wholly peaceful provisioning attempt. No doubt the truth lies somewhere in between those two positions, but much closer to the second than to the first. The truth seems to be that Lincoln, though having no intention of wantonly starting a war, was yet willing to risk one if he had to do so for the sake of the Union. He did only what, in his place, any self-respecting president, sworn to uphold the laws, would have done.[16]

This whole Fort Sumter debate has been conducted on an unfair, one-sided basis. The argument centers about Lincoln alone. He is accused — and defended. The pressures and considerations culminating in his decision are analyzed and appraised, this way and that. Yet *he* did not give the order for the firing of the first shot; Jefferson Davis did. That obvious fact somehow is overlooked. It would help to clear the air and restore our perspective if we were provided with a careful study of the pressures and considerations leading to the Confederate decision. We already have a classic anti-Lincoln essay entitled "Lincoln and Fort Sumter." What we need is a comparable article bearing some such title as "The Confederates and the First Shot."

Though there is some wasted motion in Lincoln studies, as in much of the arguing about Sumter, these studies as a whole do move on. Sweeping progress has been made. An idea of the extent of the advance can be obtained by comparing a recent synthesis with a couple of earlier ones. A generation ago the finest version of the "public Lincoln" was thought to be Lord Charnwood's slim biography (1917). One of the best accounts of the "private Lincoln" was said to be Nathaniel W. Stephenson's short volume with the long title *Lincoln: An Account of His Personal Life, Especially of Its Springs of Action as Revealed and Deepened by the Ordeal of War* (1922). Now, compare these books with the one-volume biography written by the late Benjamin P. Thomas (1952). The contrast is startling indeed. Charnwood's life, despite its enduring qualities, seems today rather elementary and uninformative. Stephenson's life, now wholly superseded, appears to be what indeed it is — an expertly written but mistily conceived and subjective book, one that prefers fact to falsehood only when the one fits as well as the other into the author's preconceptions, and rather fantastic preconceptions at that. Ben Thomas's book, bringing together the best researches, including his own, presents Lincoln very much as he must have been, and presents him in a well-informed and well-proportioned setting.[17]

As we look to the future, however, we can be sure that the ultimate Lincoln biography has not been written. Nor will it ever be. With respect to Lincoln studies, that is about the only thing we can be sure of. Randall's concluding words in his 1936 essay are still apt for this report of 1960: "What further products the historical guild will produce and what advances in Lincoln scholarship will appear fifty years hence . . . can only be imagined." For several years to come, with the more or less artificial stimulus of the continuing Civil War centennial observances, books and articles dealing at least tangentially with Lincoln can be expected to pour forth in unprecedented numbers. Sooner or later the output must fall off somewhat. But there is no reason to suppose that interest in Lincoln will be any less a quarter-century from now than it was a quarter-century ago.

In the future, Lincoln studies will be furthered only to a limited extent by the discovery of previously unknown Lincoln manuscripts. New documents in his handwriting do appear from time to time, and they will keep on coming to light. There are crannies in old attics and old courthouses still to be searched. Most of the findings will be of especial value to people with an antiquarian point of view, yet some of the manuscripts may add details interesting to the historian. It would be surprising, though welcome, if any broadly significant batch of Lincoln letters should yet be found.

Lincoln scholarship will be advanced mainly by the further exploitation of manuscript collections and other sources whose existence already is known. What is needed in some cases is no more than a careful restudy of materials which in the past have been rather heedlessly used. What is needed in other cases is a historian's instinct that can locate fruitful items in unsuspected places, or a historian's imagination that can see new patterns of meaning in evidence already familiar.

The motives that impel the writer of Lincoln studies are not easy to explain. Perhaps he is after the money or the acclaim that the large Lincoln public can provide. Such an explanation, for all its cynicism, may very well apply to certain individuals, but it begs the more fundamental question of why the large Lincoln public exists in the first place. Probably both author and public find in the study of the man much the same challenge and inspiration.

The essence of this appeal is elusive, yet no one at all acquainted with Lincoln will doubt its reality. As part of the appeal, there are the externals of his life — his remarkable rise as a self-made man, his association with the grand if not entirely glorious events of the republic's grimmest years, and then his martyrdom at the very hour of hard-won victory. There are the mysteries about him — the strange reticences and silences in the record, the controversies that call for additional study and for additional controversy. More important, there are his inner qualities — the humor and the sadness, the essential humanity, the basic integrity and incorruptibility that resist all debunking, all scholarly prying, and that generation after generation cause those who know him best to admire him most. Finally, and perhaps most important, there is his aspect as the personification of democracy — the living symbol, the perfect exponent, whose eloquence goes to the heart of the democratic dilemma and thus gives him a perpetual timeliness, an eternal relevance to the problems of popular government.

NOTES

1. Carl Sandburg, *Abraham Lincoln: The War Years* (New York: Harcourt, Brace, 1939); J. G. Randall, *Lincoln the President* (New York: Dodd, Mead, 1945-55), vol. 4 completed by Richard N. Current; David C. Mearns, *The Lincoln Papers: The Story of the Collection, with Selections to July 4, 1861* (Garden City, N.Y.: Doubleday, 1948); Roy P. Basler, Marion Dolores Pratt, and Lloyd A. Dunlap, eds., *The Collected Works of Abraham Lincoln* (New Brunswick, N.J.: Rutgers University Press, 1953-55); David Donald, ed., *Inside Lincoln's Cabinet: The Civil War Diaries of Salmon P. Chase* (New York: Longmans, Green, 1954); Howard K. Beale and Alan W. Brownsword, eds., *The Diary of Gideon Welles, Secretary of the Navy under Lincoln and Johnson* (New York: Norton, 1960).

2. Benjamin P. Thomas, *Portrait for Posterity: Lincoln and His Biographers* (New Brunswick, N.J.: Rutgers University Press, 1947).

3. Albert A. Woldman, *Lawyer Lincoln* (Boston: Houghton Mifflin, 1936); John J. Duff, *A. Lincoln, Prairie Lawyer* (New York: Rinehart, 1960).

4. Ruth Painter Randall, *Mary Lincoln: Biography of a Marriage* (Boston: Little, Brown, 1953) and *The Courtship of Mr. Lincoln* (Boston: Little, Brown, 1957).

5. David Donald, *Lincoln's Herndon* (New York: Knopf, 1948).

6. Donald W. Riddle, *Congressman Abraham Lincoln* (Urbana: University of Illinois Press, 1957).

7. William E. Baringer, *Lincoln's Rise to Power* (Boston: Little, Brown, 1937).

8. William B. Hesseltine, *Lincoln and the War Governors* (New York: Knopf, 1948).

9. Harry J. Carman and Reinhard H. Luthin, *Lincoln and the Patronage* (New York: Columbia University Press, 1943).

10. David Donald, *Lincoln Reconsidered: Essays on the Civil War Era* (New York: Knopf, 1956).

11. Allan Nevins, *Ordeal of the Union, 1847-1857* (New York: Scribner's, 1947), *The Emergence of Lincoln* (New York: Scribner's, 1950), and *The Statesmanship of the Civil War* (New York: Macmillan, 1953).

12. T. Harry Williams, *Lincoln and His Generals* (New York: Knopf, 1952). For a somewhat different view, see T. Harry Williams, *Lincoln and the Radicals* (Madison: University of Wisconsin Press, 1941).

13. Robert V. Bruce, *Lincoln and the Tools of War* (Indianapolis: Bobbs-Merrill, 1956).

14. Frank Maloy Anderson, *The Mystery of "A Public Man": A Historical Detective Story* (Minneapolis: University of Minnesota Press, 1948).

15. See William F. Zornow, *Lincoln and the Party Divided* (Norman: University of Oklahoma Press, 1954).

16. David M. Potter, *Lincoln and His Party in the Secession Crisis*

(New Haven: Yale University Press, 1942); Kenneth M. Stampp, *And the War Came: The North and the Secession Crisis, 1860-1861* (Baton Rouge: Louisiana State University Press, 1950).

17.   Benjamin P. Thomas, *Abraham Lincoln* (New York: Knopf, 1952). See also Reinhard H. Luthin, *The Real Abraham Lincoln* (Englewood Cliffs, N.J.: Prentice-Hall, 1960).

[IV]

Through India
with Abraham Lincoln

A S YOU APPROACH India by air, flying eastward toward Delhi, you cross the Sindi desert, which from above looks something like our state of Nevada but is even more desolate — a bit like the moon as seen through a powerful telescope. Once past the desert, you see occasional clusters of mud huts and fields enclosed by low mud walls. If you fly on from Delhi southeast to Calcutta, you see below you the broad, flat, green plain of the Ganges Valley, dotted more thickly with mud villages, and in the distance to the north you make out something that looks at first like a cloud bank with the sun glistening on it, until you notice that it does not move or change as clouds do, and finally you realize that it is the Himalayan mountain range, reaching higher than anything you ever imagined on earth. From Calcutta back across the subcontinent southwestward to Bombay, you fly over the central tableland, obscured by a haze of dust, and then past the hideous, jagged rocks of a low mountain range known as the Western Ghats. Continuing your zigzag journey, and crossing the country to the southeast again, you reach Madras, which, like Calcutta and Bombay, is on

Commencement address, sixty-ninth commencement, Lincoln Memorial University, Harrogate, Tennessee, June 6, 1960. Reprinted by permission from the *Lincoln Herald* 62 (Winter 1960): 161-65.

a low coastal plain which fringes the central plateau, and which, with its palm trees, has quite a tropical appearance.

That is a quick, bird's-eye view of India. If you saw only the airports of the large cities, you would imagine that this was a modern, progressive, and prosperous country, very much like the United States. You know better as soon as you leave the airport and head for town. Of course, you see automobiles and trucks, factories and mills, office buildings, and the like; but you also see — and smell — many things to remind you that you are a stranger in a strange land. You pass long strings of bullock carts on the road. You find cows everywhere — for cows are sacred and must not be killed or eaten — cows roaming in the streets, cows standing or lying on the streetcar tracks even in a great city like Calcutta. You are overrun by beggars and hawkers. You find indescribable poverty and filth. You smell strong spices, cooking oils, and perfumes as they mingle with the odor of stale urine and burning cow dung, which is used for fuel. You are never out of sight of people, swarms of people, the women in colorful saris, the men in Western clothes or in native dhotis. You meet a few fabulously rich people as well as the multitudes of the unbelievably poor, and you come upon occasional mansions as well as the many squalid huts. You behold the Taj Mahal, like a dream of loveliness carved in white marble; you view ancient Hindu temples, covered with stone carvings of gods and of men and women and animals so lifelike that you almost expect them to start moving about.

India is a land of extremes: beauty and filth, riches and poverty, learning and ignorance. There are endless rains in the monsoon season, and there is unbearable heat before the rains come. India is one of the oldest countries in the world, and at the same time one of the newest; for some of the most ancient traces of civilization are to be found there, and yet India became an independent nation in the modern world only in 1947. Almost anything you might say about that country of contrasts would be true. It would certainly be true to say that, on the whole, India is very different from the United States, very different in superficial and in fundamental ways, including the very outlook upon living. In India, Hinduism teaches that the highest desire is the desire for nothingness, for escape from life, escape from the dreary cycle of birth and death and reincarnation, and then birth and death and reincarnation all over again. Hinduism is a religion of passivity and pessimism. Quite different is Christianity, of course. In the Christian countries of Europe and America we are taught to strive and to hope, for success in this life as well as eternal salvation in the next.

To an American, then, India is indeed a foreign place. And yet he soon feels at home if he has Abraham Lincoln for a traveling companion, as in a sense I did during my visit there in 1959. The United States Information Service was then observing, throughout the world, the sesquicentennial of Lincoln's birth. On one of the U.S.I.S. programs I spent three months in India, traveled 10,000 miles, and made 77 appearances before schools, colleges, literary societies, Rotary clubs, and other groups. When I first arrived in the country, Indian friends assured me I would have no trouble in "selling" Lincoln to the Indian people. That proved to be the case. On a train it was easy to strike up a conversation about Lincoln with whoever happened to share my compartment. All educated Indians have heard of him and know something about him. They admire him. Indeed, they have the same sort of respect for our great national hero that we have for theirs, for Mahatma Gandhi, the father of modern India, who (like Lincoln in 1865) was assassinated at the very moment of his great triumph, in 1948.

Now, Lincoln and Gandhi were in some ways as different as their respective countries. The tall, gangling Lincoln was as typically American as the Kentucky and Indiana backwoods and the Illinois prairies from which he came. The short, bespectacled Gandhi was as typically Indian as the dhoti he wore (which in American cartoons looked much like a diaper). Both of these men represent the finest in their respective cultures, and both appeal to people of very different cultural backgrounds. The universal appeal of Lincoln and Gandhi is due in part to the fact that both were truly great men, and such men have some of the same essential qualities of humanity; they belong to the entire world and not merely to the country in which they happen to be born. But Lincoln appeals to Indians (and Gandhi to Americans) also because there are certain broad similarities in Indian and American history and in the historical roles of the two men.

Let me mention a few of the similarities in the history of India and America. First, both countries once were British colonies, and both gained independence after a hard struggle, the one in 1776 and the other in 1947. A small reminder of this common experience is the fact that there are streets named Cornwallis in both Greensboro, North Carolina, and Calcutta. Lord Cornwallis, who fought a battle in the Revolutionary War near the present site of Greensboro, afterward served as viceroy of India. A second historical parallel: the United States and India launched their independent careers as comparatively weak countries in a world of brutal and dangerous power politics, and for their own safety both tried to avoid entanglement in the power struggles that threatened them. With respect to India, this policy is known as "neutralism"; with respect to the United States, as "isolationism." Third, the United States at one time suffered from sectionalism, which finally led to secession and the Civil War. India experienced a kind of disunion in 1947, when the country was partitioned and the separate nation of Pakistan was set up. Partition was accompanied by considerable bloodshed, as "communal riots" broke out between Hindus and Muslims. India continues to be torn by divisive forces — "fissiparous tendencies," they are called there — forces comparable to the sectionalism in the United States more than a century ago. The fourth historical parallel: America and India have a comparable record of inhumanity to particular groups. In the United States there is the Negro, who once was held as private property. According to the Constitution, as recently interpreted, he is entitled to the same public facilities as other people. In fact, however, he has yet to be accepted as an equal. In India there is the person of the lower castes and especially of the outcastes or "untouchables." He is declared, in the new Indian constitution, to be entitled to the same rights and privileges as anyone else. But in fact the low-caste person in India, like the Negro in the United States, is still the victim of various kinds of discrimination.

These parallels between India and America might be summarized by saying that in both countries freedom and equality are goals that have been imperfectly achieved, but in both countries serious efforts are under way to make democracy work. Lincoln and Gandhi, in their different historical settings, stood for the ideals expressed in our Declaration of Independence, the ideals of national unity, personal freedom, and equality of opportunity. So it is not surprising that many Indians — even Gandhi himself — should have found inspiration in the life of a man from the remote American frontier, different though that man and his surroundings were, in so many ways, from the Indian experience.

Naturally, the acquaintance of Indians with Lincoln varies a great deal. Probably most of the villagers, ignorant and uneducated, who comprise the vast majority of the population, never heard of him — or, for that matter, of the United States. Others know little more than his name, and they think of him as a kind of "guru," or holy man. But those educated in schools or colleges under the British regime invariably know him, mainly through the famous play, "Abraham Lincoln," written by the Englishman John Drinkwater. (As a junior-high-school boy in Colorado, I too read that play, and thus possessed a common experience that created a bond of understanding with many of the Indians I met.) There are Indian university professors who are well acquainted with Lincoln, with our Civil War, and with American history as a whole; they can discuss these subjects with sophistication and authority. In New Delhi, the national capital, there is even an Abraham Lincoln Society; it has regular quarters in a handsome building, and it maintains a respectable collection of writings on Lincoln. The leaders of this society are Indians, not Americans. The society observed Lincoln's Birthday in 1959 with a symposium in which prominent Indians discussed the general subject of civil rights.

Informed Indians, as one might expect, often make comparisons between Lincoln and Gandhi. The contrast which usually comes out is that Gandhi stood preeminently for nonviolence, for the achievement of national independence and other goals by *satyagraha*, or passive resistance. Though Lincoln, too, was a man of peace, he had to use force to save the Union, and he is known as a great war leader. In the comparisons that Indians make, Lincoln usually comes off second best, as might be expected. He keeps up pretty well in the race until the final curve and the home stretch, then is left behind in the dust, while Gandhi goes on to be classed with Buddha and with Jesus Christ. Yet I talked with more than one Indian who thought that Lincoln was greater than Gandhi. One man assured me that, if India had had a Lincoln in 1947, there might or might not have been a civil war but there would have been no partition, no separate state of Pakistan. Gandhi permitted secession; Lincoln did not.

Lincoln, as well as Gandhi, is to Indians a leading exponent of democratic philosophy. These people are trying to adapt to their way of life the essential elements of democracy as it exists in Western Europe and the United States. The democratic-minded Indians are quite aware that, unless they soon can make a going thing of democracy, communism may become a real danger. Certainly an undercurrent of pro-communist and anti-American feeling is strong among frustrated college graduates and young intellectuals. In the present "cold war" — in the contest for the good will of the "uncommitted" nations like India — we have one very valuable asset that the Russians do not: we have an Abraham Lincoln.

Some of the thinking people in India are trying to lay down a theoretical as well as a material basis for democratic society. They are fascinated by Lincoln's classic definition: "government of the people, by the people, for the people." Time and again on my travels I was asked what Lincoln meant by each of these prepositions — "of," "by," and "for." I could not give a good explanation, and I rather doubt if Lincoln himself could have done so. I suspect that he used the three prepositional phrases largely for rhetorical effect and not with any intention of attaching some special meaning to each one.

Eventually I discovered some of the background for this extraordinary interest in Lincoln's prepositions, when an Indian political philosopher named Atulananda Chakrabarti called on me at the Calcutta hotel where I was staying. Mr. Chakrabarti had written several pamphlets, a few of which he gave me. From him and from his writings I learned that UNESCO (the United Nations Educational, Scientific, and Cultural Organization) had sponsored a discussion of the redefinition of democracy, at New Delhi in 1950. The Indian participants there had proposed adding a fourth phrase to Lincoln's famous definition, so as to make it read: "government of the people, by the people, for the people, and *with* the people."

Let me quote some scattered sentences from one of Mr. Chakrabarti's pamphlets:

> The obvious rhetorical manner in which the Lincolnian prepositions — "of," "by," and "for" — have been arrayed appears to suggest that Lincoln at the moment was in a mood more for an oration than a definition. Yet his genius was unerring. And no other political thinker has ever by any studied effort so far reached a more understandable and workable definition of democracy. . . . Of these prepositions, "by" is the most essential one. . . . Some critics thus differentiate the American and Russian democracies: "by" refers to the former, and "for," in the sense of "in the interest of," to the latter. . . . [But] "by" only means "with the consent of." . . . To complement the shortcomings of the Gettysburg dogma, Dr. Bhidan Chandra Roy, Chief Minister of West Bengal, India, simply follows up Lincoln with yet another preposition, and this one is "with." . . . Dr. Roy thinks, if democracy is to fit into the tradition . . . and express the genius of India, the Vedic preposition *sam* (together with), which is stressed in the prayer for concord of king and the people, has to be introduced.

Suppose you were asked to comment on this rather complicated discussion of prepositions and togetherness — I wonder what you would say. Well, my visitor in the Calcutta hotel, Mr. Chakrabarti, did ask my opinion, and I hardly knew what to tell him. I tried to explain that, from the American point of view, as from the Indian, Lincoln was an extremely eloquent spokesman for democracy, but that few of us looked for particular meanings in his prepositions. I tried to explain, further, that Lincoln made a noteworthy contribution to popular government by what he *did* as well as what he said. He was a practical politician, and only by being one could he become a successful statesman. It seemed to me that a working democracy must depend upon practical politics as well as high ideals — both are indispensable. It seemed to me also (though I did not say this) that here lay a possible weakness in Indian democracy. In India, perhaps too much attention is paid to words, to abstractions; not enough attention is given to the everyday realities of conducting a responsible and efficient government — whether it be of, by, for, or with the people.

In any case, this meticulous concern with Lincoln's words, even his tiniest ones, was one of many evidences I found in India that, ninety-five years after his death, Lincoln is far from forgotten. He is remembered wherever and whenever democracy is being given serious thought. Throughout the free world we shall face for a long time the task of maintaining democratic government, by democratic means, against manifold dangers that threaten from both outside and in. And so there is no reason to think that interest in Lincoln, at home or abroad, will soon decline.

I came away from India with the conviction that we Americans ourselves would be better able to face the difficulties of today's world — the world of the intercontinental missile and the hydrogen bomb — if we were more intimately acquainted with the character and career of Abraham Lincoln. We have much more to learn from his statesmanship during what were, until the present, the republic's grimmest years. We have much to learn from his inner qualities: the humor and sadness, the essential humanity, the basic integrity and incorruptibility that resist all debunking, all scholarly prying, and that generation after generation cause those who know him best to admire him most. And we have much to learn from him as a personification of democracy: the living symbol, the perfect exponent, whose eloquence goes to the heart of the democratic dilemma and thus gives him that perpetual timeliness, that eternal relevance to the problems of popular government.

[V]

The Confederates
and the First Shot

JEFFERSON DAVIS made a fateful decision on April 10, 1861. After consulting with his cabinet in Montgomery, he directed his war secretary, L. P. Walker, to order General P. G. T. Beauregard, in command of the Confederate forces at Charleston, to demand the surrender of Fort Sumter and, if the demand should be rejected, to reduce the fort. The next day Major Robert Anderson at Sumter received and rejected the demand. He remarked, however, that if the Confederates did not "batter the fort to pieces" before then, he and his men would be "starved out in a few days." Beauregard telegraphed Walker, and Walker conferred with Davis. Then Walker wired back authorizing Beauregard to "avoid the effusion of blood" if Anderson would state a time for his withdrawal and would agree meanwhile not to fire unless fired upon. Beauregard sent James Chesnut, Roger A. Pryor, and two aides by boat to present this offer to Anderson. It was already after midnight on the morning of April 12. Anderson promised to hold his fire and to evacuate in three days — unless he should receive "controlling instructions" or "additional supplies." Chesnut and

A paper read at the fifty-fourth annual meeting of the Mississippi Valley Historical Association, Detroit, Michigan, April 19, 1961. Reprinted by permission from *Civil War History* 7 (December 1961): 357-69.

Pryor informed him that his reply was unsatisfactory and that the Confederate batteries would begin bombarding in an hour.

Instead of taking such responsibility upon themselves, these hotheaded underlings might have referred Anderson's reply to Beauregard, and he in turn to Walker and Davis. Upon this might-have-been of history a fair amount of thought and ink has been wasted. Davis might have accepted Anderson's conditions, but he himself never gave any indication that he would have done so. Quite the contrary. He afterward wrote that "the 'controlling instructions' were already issued" and "the 'additional supplies' were momentarily expected"; so there was "obviously no other course to be pursued" than the course the Confederates pursued that morning.[1] The basic decision was Davis's, and to the last he stuck by it.

Why he did so, considering the risks and dangers he thus brought upon his beloved South, is a question that has never been fully answered and perhaps can never be. His own justification — that "the reduction of Fort Sumter was a measure of defense rendered absolutely and immediately necessary" — is unconvincing. Sumter offered no immediate threat to the physical safety of Charleston or of South Carolina — or of the other six states that then composed the Confederacy. Designed as a protection against seaborne invasion, the fort exposed its weak side to the Confederates on land. Still under construction, it was thinly manned and poorly gunned. As a possible danger to the Confederates, it was more than offset by the shore batteries constructed around it and aimed at it. Once the firing had in fact begun, these batteries practically demolished its walls. With his smoothbores firing round shot, Anderson could not hurt the Confederates; they were beyond his effective range.[2]

Long before the Sumter guns were thus put to the test, Davis himself had acknowledged their inability to harm the Charlestonians. In January, writing to Governor Francis W. Pickens of South Carolina, he counseled that Sumter be left alone. "The little garrison in its present position," he explained, "presses on nothing but a point of pride."[3] The little garrison in its April position pressed still less on anything but pride, for by April the Confederate batteries had been vastly strengthened. On April 12 there was no immediate overriding military peril that compelled the Confederates to open fire.

The approach of a small fleet, under Captain Gustavus Vasa Fox, created no such peril. President Lincoln had made clear, in the notice he sent by personal messenger to Governor Pickens, that the expedition was only bringing supplies to the hungry garrison and would attempt no more unless that much were to be resisted. These supplies, if landed without opposition, would not have changed the balance, or imbalance, of the forces facing one another in Charleston harbor. Even additional arms, ammunition, and troops, if there had been any possibility that the Sumter expedition could have successfully landed them, would have made little difference in the military situation.

In justifying his policy, Davis charged the Lincoln administration with a deceptive maneuver. He contended that the Confederate commissioners in Washington had been "receiving assurances calculated to inspire hope in the success of their mission," and that President Lincoln and Secretary William H. Seward had "profited by the delay created by their own assurances, in order to prepare secretly the means for effective hostile operations."[4] In truth, neither the commissioners nor Davis was deceived. As his own war secretary wrote to Beauregard on April 2, "The government [at Montgomery] has at no time placed any reliance on assurances by the government at Washington in respect to the evacuation of Fort Sumter, or entertained any confidence in the disposition of the latter to make any concession or yield any point to which it is not driven by absolute necessity."[5]

Actually, the commissioners thought they were using Seward, rather than he them. They knew that he personally favored concession and delay. They were aware of his belief that, given time, Southerners would rebel against the rebellion and bring the seceded states back into the Union. The wily commissioners encouraged him in this hope, for they were quite willing "to play with Seward, to delay and gain time until the South was ready."[6] Eventually, even before Lincoln had announced his plan to provision Sumter, they concluded that the day had come to abandon their game.

All along, for weeks before the Sumter incident, the seceded states and the Confederate government had been making aggressive and warlike moves. South Carolina had "fired the first gun" as early as January 8, when the unarmed merchant steamer *Star of the West* arrived in Charleston harbor with provisions which, because of the menace from the shore batteries, never got to Sumter. As the cotton states, one after another, revolted against the Union, the secessionists within each state proceeded to take, by force or the threat of force when necessary, all the forts, arsenals, mints, customhouses, and other federal property within their reach. While delegates were on their way to the Montgomery convention to set up the Confederacy, they rejoiced to learn that two more United States forts and an arsenal, "all on Alabama soil," had fallen.[7] Soon after the Montgomery Congress convened, its members resolved that "immediate steps should be taken to obtain possession of forts Sumter and Pickens . . . either by negotiation or [by] force."[8] Carrying the resolution into effect, Davis sent his commissioners to Washington for negotiation. He sent other agents to the North and to Europe to buy arms — in case negotiation should fail.

In early March, Davis issued a call for 100,000 volunteers for one year's service; within a few weeks the Confederate States Army numbered 35,000 men — twice as many as its federal counterpart. Meanwhile, politicians in the lower South grew impatient with the efforts of the commissioners in Washington. "These men should require to know within five days whether the forts on our soil, and justly belonging to us, are to be given up," a Savannah newspaper insisted early in April, "or whether we shall be compelled to take them by force of arms."[9] Already state troops were descending upon Pensacola in preparation for an attack against Fort Pickens. "Mobile looks more like a military barracks than a commercial city," the fire-eater Howell Cobb reported while visiting there on March 31. "There are some fifteen hundred troops here on their way to Pensacola — most of them from Mississippi and composed of the best young men of the State."[10]

While the embattled Confederates pressed on to capture one point after another, the federal government under President Buchanan and then under President Lincoln showed remarkable patience and forbearance. But the secessionists were far from being appeased. They denounced alike the irresolute Buchanan and the cautious Lincoln as menaces to peace. Davis, while yet a senator from Mississippi, railed against the Buchanan administration for permitting an "act of hostility" when Anderson made bold to transfer his garrison from the vulnerable Fort Moultrie to the somewhat more defensible Fort Sumter. Soon afterward Davis wrote privately that the incoming Lincoln would "have but to continue in the path of his predecessor to inaugurate a civil war."[11]

Throughout February and March, while pretending that their own proceedings were "acts of peace and gentleness," the Deep South leaders spoke indignantly of federal plotting to "coerce" them. These men took the strange position, as the Nashville *Republican Banner* pointed out, that the "Congress of the Cotton States" had the right, "by force of arms, *to coerce and destroy the Federal Government*," and that if the federal government should directly or indirectly resist, "*the act* of resistance and self-defense" would be "coercion by the Federal Government of the revolutionary Cotton States! Well, black may be white, wrong may be right, and night may be day. . . ."[12] The Confederates took another and equally curious position, namely, that they should be allowed day after day to add to their power and possessions with impunity, while Lincoln must do nothing to upset the status quo in the slightest. If he dared do anything, he must bear the obloquy for bringing on a war.

As has been seen, the Confederates struck at Sumter when Lincoln took a step they could have looked upon as merely an effort to preserve the status quo. Very likely they would have struck somewhere, sometime, even if he had dealt with the Confederate commissioners in Washington and had yielded to all their demands — even if he had given up Sumter and, along with it, Pickens and the rest of the places which, as late as April 12, federal forces still occupied within the boundaries the Confederacy claimed. For not one of the Confederate leaders was satisfied with the boundaries as drawn at that time. Not one had a vision so narrow as to embrace, in the emerging nation of the South, no more than the string of seven states whose representatives had foregathered in Montgomery. Rather, these would-be nation-builders had grand, imperial designs which could not well be achieved without considerable bloodshed.

At the very least, as the most moderate of the Confederate imperialists envisaged it, the full-grown Confederate States of America would have to include Virginia and the other slaveholding commonwealths of the upper South and the border. More than that, in the opinion of some advocates of a united South the new nation must obtain the District of Columbia and a share of all federal territories and federal property. If all the slave states came together, the New Orleans *Picayune* predicted on the day that South Carolina seceded, the "line forming their northern border" would be above all the territory "adapted to the extension of slavery." A large part of the West thus would be "at the control of the united South. . . . More than this, we absolutely carry with us . . . the District of Columbia, with all the millions of national property within its limits." In addition, the Confederacy of the future "holds the mouth of the Mississippi and has the keys to the commerce of the entire Mississippi and Ohio valley."[13]

Sharing the glorious vision of the New Orleans *Picayune,* the Charlottesville *Review* on January 25, 1861, declared: "Of course we come forward to claim our share of the general property. We must have a division of the public domain; we must have the city of Washington with its numerous and costly public buildings, as lying within the area of the Southern Confederacy; we must have the fortifications in the Florida Keys, which command the navigation of the Gulf of Mexico; we must have the right to establish strict police regulations on the Mississippi River."[14] From the Gulf of Mexico the new empire, in the dreams of prominent Confederates, would stretch all the way to the Pacific Ocean, so as to include the territories of Colorado, New Mexico, Utah, and Arizona, and even the state of California, to say nothing of eventual accretions that might come from Mexico, Central America, and the Caribbean islands.

In the minds of at least a few of its leaders, the Confederacy had possibilities of expansion to the north, beyond the free-state border, as well as to the west and south. Though Vice-President Alexander Stephens had spoken of the idea of racial inequality and Negro slavery as the "cornerstone" of the Confederacy, he came to foretell the early admission of the free states of the Northwest and to refer to prospects of "reorganization and new assimilation." Some of his fellow Confederates understood Stephens to mean that, eventually, the new nation might also accept Pennsylvania, New York, and most of the members of the old nation. The once-proud United States would then amount to little.[15]

At the beginning of April, 1861, none of these imperial ambitions had been realized, and none appeared to be on the way to early realization. Virginia remained aloof from the Confederacy. On April 4 the Virginia convention, which had been elected to consider secession, voted 89 to 45 against it. Until Virginia left the Union, no other slave state was likely to do so. Thus it was doubtful (unless something drastic was done) whether additional states would leave the Union.

Indeed, it was doubtful whether all the seceded seven would stay out — and stay together. A desire to return to the Union seemed especially strong in Alabama, the very home of the Confederate government. If, among prominent Confederates, true Unionists or "Reconstructionists" were few, men of dubious Southernism were numerous. They were far too numerous for fire-eaters like Robert Barnwell Rhett, who suspected most of the Montgomery statesmen, including Davis and above all Stephens.

"We are in danger," Rhett's organ, the Charleston *Mercury,* warned on March 25, ". . . of being dragged back eventually to the old political affiliations with the States and peoples from whom we have just cut loose."[16]

Superficial and unreal was the impression of unity that the Confederate founding fathers gave to outsiders. Underneath the surface, the tensions of personal rivalry and political difference were straining the newly founded nation, threatening to tear it apart. Old Whigs and old Democrats, former unionists or "cooperationists," early and determined secessionists, advocates and opponents of reopening the African slave trade — these were some of the contending groups. A sense of frustration was widespread. This was made worse by economic as well as political uncertainty. Bankers were suspending specie payments, planters and traders were bearing an increased burden of debt, and manufacturers faced a business slowdown. Time did not appear to be on the side of the Confederacy; its prospects deteriorated with delay. There was a "feeling that the existing suspense and apprehension were intolerable, and that almost any change would be an improvement."[17] Something had to be done, and soon.

War might be the thing — so it seemed to unsympathetic commentators in the North. In reporting the departure of Lincoln's Sumter expedition, the Indianapolis *Daily Journal* on April 11 predicted that Lincoln's "peace policy" was about to end in hostilities.

> Why? Not because it assails anybody. Not because it coerces anybody. But because the seceding States are determined to have war; because they believe a war will drive to their support the border slave States, and unite them all in a great Southern Confederacy. A policy of peace is to them a policy of destruction. It encourages the growth of a reactionary feeling. It takes out of the way all the pride and resentment which could keep the people from feeling the weight of taxation, and the distress of their isolated condition. It forces them to reason, and to look at the consequences of their conduct. A war buries all these considerations in the fury and glory of battle, and the parade and pomp of arms. War will come because

the Montgomery government deems it the best way of bringing in the border States, and of keeping down trouble at home.[18]

If the Indianapolis *Daily Journal* was biased, the fact nevertheless remains that many voices for war were being raised in the South. "We hold that it is utterly impossible to have a peaceable dismemberment of the confederation [that is, the United States]," the New Orleans *Daily True Delta* had said as far back as December 9, 1860. "We do not stop to argue the question whether a state has the undoubted right to separate herself . . . still, is it not obvious that after her separation, she must either relinquish all pretension, all claim, all right to participate equally in the national property, public domain, improvements of all kinds, army, navy and appurtenances, etc., or prepare herself to vindicate her demands for her share by a resort to force?" This New Orleans paper added: "We do not . . . doubt their [the Southern states'] perfect ability, albeit greatly inferior, numerically, . . . to conquer a successful peace."[19]

And the Charlottesville *Review* of January 25, 1861, after listing the claims of the seceding states, went on to ask: "Does anyone suppose that all or any one of these things will be yielded by the North? We deliberately dissolve our connection with the General Government, and leave it, in their opinion, a just claim to this property, and an army and navy to defend that claim. The result will be, that they will make no war on us, but we will be forced to make war on them; or else ignominiously resign all our just and equitable claims."[20]

Some Southerners advocated what nowadays might be called "preventive war." The fiercely secessionist Richmond *Enquirer* urged, as early as December 18, the need for immediate action.

> This matter comes home to Virginia, in the disposition of Fortress Monroe. Shall the fortress remain in the hands of our enemies? . . . But to deliver over to Lincoln the defenses of the States is to offer him opportunities of aggression, and to aid in producing civil war. It is the duty of every patriot to embarrass the new administration at every point; to deprive those who have produced the

present state of affairs of all means to further involve the country in civil war. The inauguration should be prevented by Maryland, and, if necessary, Virginia should aid her.[21]

More to the point, in confirming the analysis of the Indianapolis *Daily Journal,* are expressions of Southern opinion in favor of striking a blow specifically at Fort Sumter. Among Confederates and secessionists it had become an axiom, before April 12, that violence at Sumter would automatically bring over Virginia and other slave states and thus would save the Confederacy. Above all others, the South Carolinians themselves were devoted to this doctrine, and from January on Rhett in his son's Charleston *Mercury* beat the drum for seizing the fort. The Virginia secessionists Roger A. Pryor and Edmund Ruffin went to Charleston to egg on the Carolinians. On April 10, two days before his middle-of-the-night negotiations with Major Anderson, the rabble-rousing Pryor addressed a crowd from the balcony of the Charleston Hotel. "As sure as tomorrow's sun will rise upon us, just so sure will old Virginia be a member of the Southern Confederacy; and I will tell your Governor what will put her in the Southern Confederacy in less than an hour by Shrewsbury clock. Strike a blow!"[22]

That same day Senator Louis Wigfall of Texas, then in Charleston, dispatched a telegram to his friend Jefferson Davis: "General Beauregard will not act without your order. Let me suggest to you to send the order to him to begin the attack as soon as he is ready. Virginia is excited by the preparations, and a bold stroke on our side will complete her purposes. Policy and prudence are urgent upon us to begin at once."[23] And Senator Jere Clemens of Alabama, calling upon Davis in Montgomery, overheard an Alabama leader say to War Secretary Walker: "It must be done. Delay two months, and Alabama stays in the Union. You must sprinkle blood in the faces of the people."[24]

If Clemens heard or remembered incorrectly, the idea he reported was familiar enough among Alabama leaders. Several weeks earlier one of them had privately written that there was danger to the Confederate cause in that the Republicans might back down and agree to compromise. "Our only reliance is in the manhood or imprudence of the Black Republicans," this Alabaman believed. "There is another way of avoiding the calamity of reconstruction and that is war. . . . Now pardon me for suggesting that South Carolina has the power of putting us beyond the reach of reconstruction by taking Fort Sumter at any cost."[25]

Similar views might be quoted at length. These were, of course, the views of extremists. There can be no doubt that the great majority of Southerners, people and politicians alike, desired continued peace. Such was the conclusion of Stephen A. Hurlbut, the secret emissary whom Lincoln sent to Charleston late in March. A Charlestonian by birth, Hurlbut visited with relatives and with James L. Petigru, whom he considered the only unionist left in Charleston. In his confidential report to Lincoln, Hurlbut doubtless reflected Petigru's conversation. "The power in that State [South Carolina] and in the Southern Confederacy is now in the hands of the Conservatives — of men who desire no war, seek no armed collision, but hope and expect peaceable separation, & believe that after separation the two sections will be more friendly than ever." Yet he added, "it is equally true that there exists a large minority indefatigably active and reckless who desire to precipitate collision, inaugurate war & unite the Southern Confederacy by that means. These men dread the effects of time & trial upon their Institutions." They are motivated in part by concern over the "differences between the several [Confederate] states which will be obliterated by . . . war."[26]

Though peace was the hope of most Confederates, "peace" was and is a tricky word. At the very least the Confederates expected to get all the slave states and the federal property within them. All this they longed for — all this and peace, too. Possibly they would have remained friendly enough with the old Union if President Lincoln had only consented to a treaty yielding every last one of their demands. In the South of early 1861, the concept of "peace" had this general connotation and also a different and special meaning. According to the reasoning of some Confederates, a blow at

Sumter would lead not to war but to just the opposite: it would provide a guarantee against general hostilities. As Rhett's biographer has explained, "Rhett had never believed that the North would make war upon a united South, and he did not now [when Fort Sumter was attacked] realize the struggle which was impending. The call to arms he hailed for its psychological effect: Virginia and the border states were moving toward the Confederacy, and their action would command peace."[27]

With so much confusion of terms in the air, it is not surprising that Southern statesmen, Jefferson Davis among them, engaged in a certain amount of double talk, either consciously or unconsciously. The New Orleans *Daily True Delta,* frankly accepting the necessity for force, deplored the inconsistency of some of "the more warlike" in the South.

> We censure the parties that are fanning into a flame the passions of the people, who are preparing their hearts for revolution, who are sharpening sword-blades, yet are delusively shouting peace, peace, where there is no peace. [We cannot] doubt the sincerity of the Rhetts, the Toombses, the Yanceys, and the Jeff. Davises, when they welcome, in exultant tones, the prospect of war with their countrymen . . . what we deprecate is the perpetual assurance given by them that no civil war can originate in their revolutionary schemes. . . .[28]

It appears that, indeed, Davis did blow hot and cold, did talk alternately of war and of peace. In his farewell address to the United States Senate he spoke soberly enough. On the way to Montgomery, for his inauguration there, he grew a bit bellicose in the remarks he made at some of his train's station stops. At Stevenson, Alabama, according to Southern newspaper reports, he seemed to welcome hostilities. "Your border states will gladly come into the Southern Confederacy within sixty days, as we will be their only friends," he was quoted as saying. "England will recognize us, and a glorious future is before us. . . . We will carry war where it is easy to advance — where food for the sword and torch await our armies in the densely populated cities. . . ."[29] At first, some of Davis's friends could not believe the report that he anticipated a long and bloody war. He assured them that he did anticipate one. In his Montgomery inaugural address, adopting once more a tone of sadness and regret, he gave the impression of hoping for peace while preparing for an "appeal to arms" as an unfortunate contingency.[30]

By April 10, the dilemma that Davis confronted had become painfully sharp, the more so because the consequences of his decision, whichever choice he might take, were so difficult to foresee. If he refused to sanction the firing on Fort Sumter, the consequences for the Confederate cause might on the whole be good, or bad. The Lincoln expedition might prove a fiasco (as, in the course of events, it was indeed to prove). Its failure could be expected to bring discredit upon the Lincoln administration and the cause of the North. The withholding of Confederate fire, moreover, would probably postpone the outbreak of general hostilities, at least for a time. This time could be used to advantage in furthering Confederate preparations for eventual war. Those were the favorable possibilities if Davis should hold back. The unfavorable ones were these: the eager South Carolinians might seize the initiative, fire on the fort regardless of orders from Montgomery, and leave Davis in an ineffectual and foolish posture. Or, assuming the Carolinians restrained themselves, the continued inaction would doubtless be accompanied by the continued demoralization and deterioration of the Confederacy.

On the other hand, if Davis went ahead and gave the order for reducing the fort, the consequences again might be either good or bad. Without question Virginia and other slave states would secede. Possibly, with the Union thus weakened and the Confederacy strengthened, the Northern people and the Lincoln administration would not dare risk a general war. Or, if they did risk it, the probable effect would be to inspirit and unite the South. And in the ensuing conflict the Confederates would presumably have many friends and the Federals many foes. Great Britain and France would side with the Confederacy. Southern sympathizers in the

North would hamper the Northern war effort. Various groups that the United States had antagonized from time to time — the Mexicans, the Mormons, the Indians — would be likely to help in winning an empire in the West. All this would be to the good.

But there were other possibilities, and these were frightening. If the Confederates fired the first shot, and if that shot led to civil war, they would labor under a moral and psychological handicap: they would have to wrestle with the burden of war guilt. And the war might possibly end in disaster for the South. Davis's secretary of state, Robert Toombs, in advising against a Sumter attack, is reputed to have said: "Mr. President, at this time it is suicide, murder, and will lose us every friend at the North. You will wantonly strike a hornet's nest which extends from mountain to ocean, and legions now quiet will swarm out and sting us to death. It is unnecessary; it puts us in the wrong; it is fatal."[31] Defeat in war would among other things mean the end of slavery, the cornerstone of the Confederate states. Voices in the South as well as the North were predicting that, if war should come, the peculiar institution would not survive. Davis himself seemed to sense its doom.[32]

Davis was a gentleman, a person of decent instincts. "He has achieved his reputation as a soldier," the New Orleans *Daily Picayune* had observed just one month before he faced his inexorable decision, "and we are sure he feels no desire to augment a fame that might content any man, by civil war. He will have much to do to restrain the eagerness of the young soldier, who is panting to flash his maiden sword upon his country's enemies. He will have something to do to restrain the rashness of the misguided enthusiast, who requires the bonds of [Southern] union to be cemented in blood. . . ."[33] At the last, however, the current proved too strong for Davis to buck. Among his cabinet advisers, Toombs alone counseled restraint; all the others insisted the time had come to act. Davis acted.

In the first flush of enthusiasm which the Sumter attack aroused in the South, events seemed to justify him. "We are prepared to fight, and the enemy is not," the Mobile *Advertiser* promptly proclaimed. "Now is the time for action, while he is yet unprepared. Let . . . a hundred thousand men . . . get over the border as quickly as they can. Let a division enter every Northern border State, destroy railroad connections to prevent concentrations of the enemy, and the desperate strait of these States, the body of Lincoln's country, will compel him to a peace — or compel his successor, should Virginia not suffer him to escape from his doomed capital."[34] By the time Davis had escaped from *his* doomed capital, he should have recognized his fatal error of 1861. But he never recognized it, or at least never admitted it. Perhaps his stubbornness and his self-righteousness — his wartime refusal to accept defeat, his postwar obsession with rationalizing his career — perhaps these things were, in some measure, the outer manifestations of an inner struggle to still the promptings of regret.

For all the shrill earnestness of his protests, the evidence strongly suggests that military necessity did not require the firing of the first shot. Political necessity required it. The very life of the Confederacy, the growth upon which that life depended, was at stake. So were the pride, the prestige, and the position of Jefferson Davis.

Of course, he has had his defenders, hordes of them, besides himself. He will have many more. Let them face frankly the question of his responsibility for beginning the bloodshed. That is where the burden of proof should rest — upon Davis's partisans. It should not rest, as it has done for much too many years, upon Lincoln's champions. After all, Lincoln did not order the opening barrage; Davis did. Biographers of Davis and historians of the Confederacy too often have evaded or obscured his role in the Sumter affair by digressing to levy accusations or innuendoes at Lincoln.[35] Studies aplenty exist of warmaking forces in the North. Realistic and thorough analyses of the war dynamism that rose up from the South are needed.

Perhaps a day will come, in the millennium of Clio, when the grace of objectivity fills every historian's heart. And perhaps, in that happy time, authorities North and South will agree that Lincoln himself, in his second inaugural, summed up the significance of April 12, 1861, about as aptly as anybody could sum it up in two sentences: "Both parties deprecated war; but one of them would *make* war rather than let the nation survive; and the other would *accept* war rather than let it perish. And the war came."[36]

NOTES

1. The familiar events of April 10-12 are well summarized by Allan Nevins in *The War for the Union* (New York: Scribner's, 1959-60), 1:67-70. The present paper approaches the subject from a position similar to that of Nevins. For Jefferson Davis's view, see his *The Rise and Fall of the Confederate Government* (New York: Appleton, 1881), 1:289.

2. Davis, *Rise and Fall*, p. 292; T. Harry Williams, *P. G. T. Beauregard: Napoleon in Gray* (Baton Rouge: Louisiana State University Press, 1954), p. 59.

3. Nevins, *War for the Union*, 1:73.

4. Davis, *Rise and Fall*, 1:280.

5. James Ford Rhodes, *History of the United States from the Compromise of 1850* (New York: Macmillan, 1893-1906), 3:339-40. See also Nevins, *War for the Union*, 1:67.

6. Samuel W. Crawford, *The Genesis of the Civil War* (New York: Macmillan, 1887), p. 333n. Crawford obtained this statement in 1870 from a firsthand source: John Forsyth, one of the Confederate commissioners.

7. J. W. DuBose, *The Life and Times of William Lowndes Yancey* (Birmingham: A. P. Smith, 1892), p. 551.

8. Rhodes, *History*, 3:295.

9. *Savannah Republican*, April 2, 1861, quoted in Nevins, *War for the Union*, 1:68.

10. Ulrich B. Phillips, ed., *The Correspondence of Robert Toombs, Alexander H. Stephens, and Howell Cobb* (Washington: Government Printing Office, 1913), p. 558.

11. Kenneth M. Stampp, *And the War Came: The North and the Secession Crisis, 1860-1861* (Baton Rouge: Louisiana State University Press, 1950), p. 82.

12. Quoted in Dwight L. Dumond, ed., *Southern Editorials on Secession* (New York: Century, 1931), pp. 485-86.

13. Ibid., pp. 353-54.

14. Ibid., pp. 418-19.

15. See Laura A. White, *Robert Barnwell Rhett, Father of Secession* (New York: Century, 1931), pp. 200-203.

16. Ibid., p. 203.

17. Horace Greeley, *The American Conflict: A History of the Great Rebellion* (Hartford, Conn.: Case, 1864), 1:450-51.

18. Howard C. Perkins, ed., *Northern Editorials on Secession* (New York: Century, 1942), 1:705-6.

19. Dumond, *Southern Editorials,* pp. 313-14.

20. Ibid., pp. 418-19.

21. Ibid., p. 345. A week later the same newspaper challenged Southern patriotism by asking: "Can there not be found men bold and brave enough in Maryland to unite with Virginians in seizing the Capitol at Washington?" (Rhodes, *History,* 3:300).

22. Crawford, *Genesis of the Civil War,* p. 305.

23. Hudson Strode, *Jefferson Davis, Confederate President* (New York: Harcourt, Brace, 1959), pp. 38-39.

24. Greeley, *American Conflict,* 1:632. A somewhat differently worded version is in Nevins, *War for the Union,* 1:68.

25. J. L. Pugh to W. P. Miles, January 24, 1861, in Miles Papers, Southern Historical Collection, University of North Carolina, Chapel Hill.

26. S. A. Hurlbut to Abraham Lincoln, March 27, 1861, in Robert Todd Lincoln Collection, Library of Congress.

27. White, *Rhett,* p. 205. Before Lincoln's inauguration a Georgia correspondent expressed a similar thought to Howell Cobb: "The prompt secession of Virginia, together with a peace policy adopted by Congress, are the only things which will prevent Lincoln, Scott and Co. from using force" (Phillips, *Correspondence,* pp. 543-44).

28. Dumond, *Southern Editorials,* pp. 313-14.

29. Ibid., pp. 462-63; Greeley, *American Conflict,* 1:415n. In later years Davis wrote that he had been "grossly misrepresented in sensational reports . . . which represented me as invoking war and threatening devastation of the North" (*Rise and Fall,* 1:231). Yet his belligerent statements were published in both Northern and Southern papers.

30. Davis, *Rise and Fall,* 1:230-31.

31. Pleasant A. Stovall, *Robert Toombs* (New York: Cassell, 1892), p. 266. Toombs's remark has been frequently quoted, though its authenticity is still questioned.

32. Rhodes, *History,* 3:279-99. See also Dumond, *Southern Editorials,* p. 446.

33. Dumond, *Southern Editorials,* pp. 482-83.

34. Greeley, *American Conflict,* 1:459n.

35. The charge against Lincoln has been repeated ever since April 1861. The classic elaboration of it is Charles W. Ramsdell, "Lincoln and Fort Sumter," *Journal of Southern History* 3 (August 1937): 259-88. Ramsdell, a competent authority on Confederate history, might appropriately have applied his talents to "Davis and Fort Sumter." Among recent works referring to the ulterior motives of Lincoln, but slighting those of Davis, are E. Merton Coulter, *The Confederate States of America, 1861-1865*

(Baton Rouge: Louisiana State University Press, 1950), pp. 33-39; Clement Eaton, *A History of the Southern Confederacy* (New York: Macmillan, 1954), pp. 27-28; and Charles P. Roland, *The Confederacy* (Chicago: University of Chicago Press, 1960), p. 31.

36. Roy P. Basler, Marion Dolores Pratt, and Lloyd A. Dunlap, eds., *The Collected Works of Abraham Lincoln* (New Brunswick, N.J.: Rutgers, 1953-55), 8:332.

〖 VI 〗

Lincoln and Thaddeus Stevens

PRESIDENT LINCOLN had not been in the White House long when Congressman Stevens called on him. Stevens wanted to protest the appointment of a fellow Pennsylvanian, Simon Cameron, to Lincoln's cabinet. He told Lincoln that Cameron was dishonest.

"You don't mean to say you think Cameron would steal?"

"Well, I don't think he would steal a red-hot stove."

Lincoln chuckled at this, and the next time he saw Cameron he repeated it to him, partly as a warning, partly as a joke. A little later Stevens reappeared at the White House and asked Lincoln why he had told Cameron. Lincoln said he had meant no harm and hadn't thought Cameon would get mad about it.

"Well," Stevens replied, "he *is* mad, good and mad, and he made me promise to retract. I will now do so. I believe I told you he would not steal a red-hot stove. I will now take that back."

Stevens was especially bitter about the appointment because Cameron, the head of an opposing faction, now held the cabinet post that he himself had hoped to get. After Lincoln's election, the friends of Stevens had done their best for him. One of them had even gone out to Springfield, Illinois, to plead Stevens's case.

Eleventh annual Robert Fortenbaugh Memorial Lecture, Gettysburg College, Gettysburg, Pennsylvania, November 19, 1972. Here published for the first time.

"I found rumors rife there," he reported to Stevens, "that you had an odious history in Penna. politics." Lincoln was quoted as saying that "Thad Stevens was too old." Stevens was then sixty-eight — seventeen years older than Lincoln.

At one time Stevens had been in a position to do a small favor for Lincoln. The two first met as convention delegates in 1848, when Lincoln was in the midst of his one term as a congressman and Stevens was about to be elected to his first. "You may possibly remember seeing me at the Philadelphia Convention — introduced to you as the lone whig star of Illinois," Lincoln wrote him a few months later. "I desire the undisguised opinion of some experienced and sagacious Pennsylvania politician, as to how the vote of that state . . . is likely to go." The "experienced and sagacious" Stevens obliged the modest Lincoln by responding in great detail.

The earlier careers of the two men had interesting parallels. Both were self-made men, though Stevens had the advantage of a college education, which Lincoln of course did not. Both were outsiders. They had originated in the poverty and obscurity of the backwoods, the one in Vermont, the other in Kentucky, and as young men had started afresh in new surroundings — in Pennsylvania; in Illinois. Both became successful lawyers and, as such, the advocates of business interests. In politics they kept aloof from the party of Andrew Jackson, which claimed to be the party of the common man. They joined instead the party of Henry Clay and Daniel Webster, which had to defend itself against the charge that it was the party of the rich. As Whigs, both Stevens and Lincoln stood for government aid to private enterprise by means of tariffs, subsidies, transportation improvements, and a national bank. At the same time, both found inspiration in the Declaration of Independence, which they took quite seriously as a statement of political ideals. They agreed that slavery was wrong. Nevertheless — and this is curious, in view of their later fame as emancipators — each once appeared in court, as a lawyer, to defend a slaveowner's right of property against a slave's claim to freedom.

In the very first case that Stevens argued before the supreme court of Pennsylvania, in 1821, he served as attorney for a Marylander who used to summer with his family in the Pennsylvania mountains and take along a servant named Charity Butler. According to Pennsylvania law, a slave residing six months in the state was to be considered free. When Charity Butler's summer visits had added up to more than six months, she accordingly sued for her freedom. But Stevens argued that the six months' stay must be continuous. He won the case, and Charity Butler remained a slave.

In Illinois, though the constitution prohibited slavery, the laws permitted the use of slave labor, provided the slaves were not kept permanently in the state. Robert Matson brought his blacks from Kentucky every spring to work his Illinois farm, and he took them back to Kentucky every fall. One of them, Jane Bryant, escaped from the farm in 1847 but was captured and held by the Illinois authorities. Matson, claiming her as his property, appealed to Lincoln for legal help in recovering the girl. Lincoln took the case — and lost. It was no credit to him that Jane Bryant gained her freedom.

Jane Bryant, Charity Butler — the cases of these slave women ought to cast at least a little doubt on the stories later told to adorn the theme that Lincoln and Stevens were born defenders of all the downtrodden and oppressed. There is the story of Lincoln as a young man making a flatboat trip down the Mississippi and witnessing a slave auction in New Orleans. According to the story, he was so shocked by the spectacle that he was inspired with an "unconquerable hate" for the whole institution of slavery. "If I ever get a chance to hit that thing," he swore as he walked away, "I'll hit it hard." When the chance finally came, on January 1, 1863, he struck the hated institution a death blow with his famous proclamation. Such was the basic theme of Lincoln's life — according to the history that many once were taught. As for Stevens, he provided his own rationale for his career when, at the end, he directed that he be buried among Negroes and that his gravestone bear the following epitaph: ". . . I have chosen this [burial place] that I might illustrate in death / the principles which I have advocated through a long life, / Equality of man before his Creator."

There is no need to question the sincerity of either Lincoln or Stevens. The point is merely that motivation in politics, as in the rest of life, is infinitely complex and not easily discerned. Undeterred by that, amateur psychologists have peered confidently into the psyche of the one man or the other. Each man invites psychologizing, for each was somewhat mysterious, often went in solitary ways, kept secrets to himself. Each, in his own way, had a strange appearance — Lincoln with his long, ungainly frame, his awkward gait, and his often dull, preoccupied look; Stevens with his clubfoot and limp, his completely bald head covered with a messy wig, and his habitual pout. Possibly it is true, as some have speculated, that each of the two, ill favored as he was, felt a sense of kinship with all unfortunates.

Psychological interpreters of Lincoln and Stevens have also seen great significance in the women in their lives. William H. Herndon, Lincoln's onetime law partner and later biographer, thought he could see right into the great man's "gizzard." According to Herndon, Lincoln was inspired positively by the woman he loved and negatively by the one he married. Supposedly the sad memory of the sweet Ann Rutledge sustained him ever after her untimely death had ended their youthful romance, and the all-too-real presence of the shrewish Mary Todd drove him out of the house and into the refuge of politics. (All that, of course, is a cock-and-bull story of Herndon's, and it would not be worth mentioning if it were not so widely believed.)

With regard to Stevens, a lifelong bachelor, some of his biographers have made a great deal out of the rumors and charges which his political enemies continually circulated. There was the pregnant black girl who was found dead in a field near Gettysburg, and for whose pregnancy and death Stevens was blamed. There was the friend who, after his unmarried daughter had given birth, swore out a warrant for Stevens's arrest on a charge of fornication and bastardy. And, far more important, there was the widow Lydia

Smith, a tasteful and attractive mulatto who was for twenty years his housekeeper in Lancaster and who — according to rumors he never denied — was also his mistress. Some writers have guessed that, from his love for Lydia Smith, he acquired a deep sympathy for all blacks, free and slave, and an undying hatred for the slaves' oppressors, the Southern whites.

Whatever the merit in speculations of that kind, they are hardly necessary for understanding the political course of either Lincoln or Stevens. As politicians, both men naturally aspired to get and hold and exercise the powers of public office. Their political behavior can be discussed in the light of plain ambition without regard to other more mysterious motives. Both men were certainly ambitious, and both knew what it meant to have their hopes frustrated. Stevens, long before his failure to enter Lincoln's cabinet, had been chagrined by being excluded from William Henry Harrison's. He was to hope in vain for a later appointment to Lincoln's cabinet, and also for promotion from the House of Representatives to the Senate. Lincoln, too, had been disappointed when, after Zachary Taylor's election, he failed to receive a government job he desperately wanted. Twice he was beaten as a contender for a Senate seat.

Few politicians have been noted for possessing a sense of humor. Both Lincoln and Stevens did. They sometimes used humor for political ends, and they sometimes said things that were broad and earthy — indeed, scatological and unprintable. Otherwise, they were quite different as humorists. Lincoln was always being reminded of a story, which he would relate in a genial, kindly spirit and then would laugh at uproariously himself. He used jokes to relax tension, to illustrate a point, or to beguile unwelcome visitors and make them forget what they had come for. Stevens, on the other hand, was no storyteller but a master of original and often brutal wit. He shot out his sarcastic remarks with a straight face or, at most, a grim smile. He used his jibes to intimidate his opponents — or to disconcert his friends. (After he had addressed an antislavery meeting, one of the ladies present asked him for a lock of his hair to remember him by. He took off his wig, handed it to her, and said: "Here, help yourself.")

Lincoln was not Stevens's choice for the Republican nomination in 1860. Stevens, a delegate to the Chicago convention, would have preferred Judge John McLean of the Supreme Court. The reason, oddly enough, was that Lincoln seemed too radical on the slavery question. He had said the nation could not long endure half slave and half free, and some people took this to mean that he was practically an abolitionist. McLean, by contrast, was known as one of the most conservative of Republicans. Stevens, viewing the forthcoming election strictly as a politician, thought McLean would offend fewer voters and would have a better chance of carrying the doubtful states. Once Lincoln had been nominated, Stevens campaigned strenuously for him in Pennsylvania. Only "a few old women in pantaloons," he assured his fellow Pennsylvanians, took seriously the Southern threat that a victory for Lincoln would lead to secession and perhaps to war.

After Lincoln had been elected and secession (despite Stevens's assurances) had begun, Stevens was afraid that Lincoln, once in office, would be too weak to stand up to the seceders. (One wonders what the timid and indecisive old Judge McLean would have done as president during the secession crisis.) "Rather than show repentance for the election of Mr. Lincoln, with all its consequences," Stevens declared in the House of Representatives, "I would see this Government crumble into a thousand atoms." Privately he wrote: "If, when Mr. Lincoln came into power, he should imitate [Andrew] Jackson and act vigorously about coercing obedience, the people will admire and rally again to the republican standards." If, instead, Lincoln should seek union and peace through compromise, Stevens implied, the Republican party rather than the United States government would crumble. After the inauguration the new president lived up to the hopes of Stevens and others like him. Lincoln sent his expedition to Fort Sumter, and the war came.

During the war Lincoln and Stevens saw little of one another.

Stevens never called at the White House except when he had urgent business with the president; then he found him friendly enough, as a rule. When the congressman had a favor to ask on behalf of one of his constituents, the president usually was only too glad to grant it — a job in the foreign service, a pardon, a discharge from the army. These, of course, were political rather than personal favors. As chairman of the House Ways and Means Committee — which then had powers later to be divided among three committees — Stevens was one of the most influential members of Congress. Without the support of this congressional leader, the president would have had a hard time carrying out any program, civil or military.

From the beginning Stevens disagreed with Lincoln about war methods and war aims. Stevens was one of those Republicans who were to be known as Radicals. According to "revisionist" historians, such as the late James G. Randall, the Radical Republicans were as far from Lincoln at one extreme as the Copperhead Democrats were at the other, and caused him just as much or even more trouble. According to some of the more recent historians, such as Professor Randall's student David Donald, Lincoln and the Radicals had no more serious disagreements than normally arise between a president and congressmen of his own party. Maybe so; but certainly the differences between Lincoln and Stevens at times were wide and deep.

The two men had different conceptions of the very nature of the war. Originally Lincoln took the position that it was not really a war at all; it was simply a matter of enforcing the laws, of putting down an insurrection. Yet, only a week after the firing on Fort Sumter, he issued a proclamation of blockade. Promptly Stevens went to Washington and gave the president a lecture on international law. He pointed out to Lincoln that, in peacetime, a government does not issue such a proclamation and at no time does it blockade its own ports. By implication, he went on, the president had both acknowledged the existence of a state of war and recognized the Confederacy as a belligerent. Henceforth, in law

85

as well as in fact, the Union and the Confederacy were two separate, warring nations. This being so, the American Constitution
no longer applied, but only international law, the "laws of war."

Lincoln was soon claiming and exercising the "war powers" of
the president. He and other authorities in the North eventually
adopted the theory that they were dealing with both a rebellion
and a war — the War of the Rebellion. He continued to assume
that the Constitution remained in effect with regard to the South
as well as the North, yet he did things he could not constitution-
ally have done if that had been so. In 1862, for example, he appointed military governors for Tennessee and other Southern states
that federal troops had occupied. How could he have done such
a thing if the Constitution still operated in the South? Stevens, in
a House speech, drew attention to the president's confusion. He
himself was much more logical, much more consistent. All along
he maintained that, as soon as any part of the South was occupied,
it became "conquered territory" with which the Union could do
as it pleased, subject only to the restraints of international law.

In Stevens's view the Constitution, with its guarantees of state's
rights, no longer protected slavery in the Southern states. Now
that the war was on, the federal government ought to free the slaves
and use them against the enemy. "You send forth your sons and
brothers to shoot and saber and bayonet the insurgents," Stevens
exclaimed in Congress, "but you hesitate to break the bonds of
the slave to reach the same end. What puerile inconsistency!" Conservative Republicans deplored the speech as an "attack upon the
administration of Mr. Lincoln." Certainly the administration had
given no sign that it intended to free and arm the slaves. Rather,
Lincoln was countermanding John C. Frémont and other generals
who issued emancipation proclamations on their own. Lincoln held
back because he feared the social consequences of sudden emancipation, because he hesitated to antagonize Kentucky and other
border slave states, and because he doubted whether he had constitutional authority to act.

In the summer of 1862 Stevens and other Radicals tried to force

Lincoln's hand by passing a bill authorizing the president to take the slaves of disloyal masters, set them free, and enroll them as troops. Questioning the constitutionality of the bill, Lincoln refused to sign it until it had been amended and weakened. Even then he declined to carry it out. Stevens was discouraged. The "continued refusal to receive Negro soldiers," he confided to a friend, "convince[s] me that the Administration are preparing the people to receive an ignominious surrender to the South."

In response to the growing Radicalism in Congress and throughout the North, Lincoln had begun to work out an emancipation plan of his own. If he had had his way, the slaveowners would have been compensated, the slaves would have been freed gradually (the last of them not until about 1900), and instead of being used as soldiers they would have been shipped out of the country and resettled in Africa, Haiti, or Central America. Only after he failed to muster much support for this plan did he decide on the Emancipation Proclamation. He had concluded that, on the basis of his powers as commander-in-chief, he could issue the proclamation as a war measure; so he applied it not to the loyal slave states or to the occupied parts of the South, but only to those areas where the war was still going on. Critics sneered that he was proclaiming freedom only where he could not enforce it. Nevertheless, Stevens considered the proclamation a step forward. For once he approved of what Lincoln had done.

But Lincoln continued to show a lack of enthusiasm for black troops, accepting them much more slowly than Stevens demanded. Stevens blamed this on the influence of border-state politicians — in particular, the influence of the Blair family. Old man Blair, once a member of Andrew Jackson's "kitchen cabinet," lived in Silver Spring, Maryland, just outside Washington, and still considered himself an unofficial adviser to whoever happened to be president. His son Montgomery was Lincoln's postmaster general. His other son, Francis, Jr., was both a member of Congress and a general in the army. Regarding Montgomery Blair, Stevens wrote in the fall of 1863: "If such men are to be retained in Mr. Lincoln's

Cabinet, it is time we were consulting about his [Lincoln's] successor."

While Stevens was thinking of replacing Lincoln, some of Lincoln's friends were thinking of replacing Stevens. Lincoln's preferred candidate for Speaker of the House, in the new Congress about to meet, was none other than young Frank Blair. With Blair as speaker, Stevens could not expect to continue as chairman of the Ways and Means Committee, so he was making preparations to defeat Lincoln's candidate for the speakership at the time when, in company with Secretary of State Seward (a conservative), Lincoln was taking a trip to dedicate a new national cemetery. On the day of the ceremony someone asked Stevens where Lincoln and Seward were going. "To Gettysburg," Stevens replied. "But where are [Secretary of War] Stanton and [Secretary of the Treasury] Chase?" "At home, at work," Stevens answered regarding these two Radicals. "Let the dead bury the dead." After Congress met, Stevens not only prevented Frank Blair from getting the speakership but also managed to have him expelled from the House — on the grounds that no one could simultaneously hold both a military commission and a congressional seat.

Meanwhile Lincoln and Stevens were diverging in their thoughts about the reconstruction of the Union after the war. In December 1863 the President proposed his "10 percent" plan, by which 10 percent of the voters in a seceded state could form a new government when they had sworn to obey federal laws and proclamations, including those touching upon slavery. So far as Stevens was concerned, the 10 percent plan would make reunion much too easy for the Southerners. He had been thinking of a "radical revolution," one that would "remodel our institutions," as he wrote privately. "It would involve the desolation of the South as well as emancipation; and a repeopling of half the Continent." Now he spoke out in the House against the Lincoln plan. "We may conquer rebels and hold them in subjection," he insisted, but it was a "mere mockery" of democratic principles to say that a "tithe" of a state's inhabitants could form a government because they were "more holy or more loyal than the others."

The Republicans in Congress got busy with an alternative plan, the Wade-Davis bill, which would have required a majority and not merely a tenth to take an oath of future loyalty. Stevens himself wanted something much stronger than the Wade-Davis bill: he wanted a law that would have classified the "so-called states" of the South as mere "territories" and would have confiscated all lands belonging to rebels who owned a hundred acres or more.

While the Wade-Davis bill was in the making, the Republican national convention of 1864 met in Baltimore. Stevens, again a delegate, voted for Lincoln only because there was no other realistic choice. But Stevens objected to Andrew Johnson of Tennessee, whom Lincoln secretly had picked as his preference for a running mate. Turning to a fellow delegate, Stevens muttered: "Can't you find a candidate for Vice-President in the United States without going down to one of those rebel provinces to pick one up?"

After helping to renominate Lincoln, Stevens soon joined with other Republicans in a plot to undo the nomination and take him off the ticket. These Republicans were furious with the president because he had pocket-vetoed the Wade-Davis bill, and they feared that his association with conservative advisers would make it impossible for him to win the election. Stevens now believed that Lincoln was in a hurry to reconstruct the Southern states so as to obtain their electoral votes. What Lincoln ought to do instead, Stevens thought, was to clean up his cabinet by eliminating Montgomery Blair. On a hot August day Stevens called on Lincoln and told him so, but he got no satisfaction. After returning to Lancaster he was heard to say: "If the Republican party desires to succeed, they must get him off the track and nominate a new man." Only after Blair's resignation was announced in September did Stevens begin to campaign wholeheartedly for Lincoln.

As the war was drawing to a close, Lincoln spoke "with malice toward none, with charity for all," of "binding up the nation's wounds." Stevens was talking of forcing the Southerners to "eat the fruit of foul rebellion." Late in March 1865 he went to the White House to caution the president against making too hasty and too easy a peace. Lincoln looked at him awhile in silence. "Stevens," he finally said, "this is a pretty big hog we are trying to catch, and to hold when we do catch him." It was the last time they saw each other.

When Stevens died, Lincoln had been dead for only three years but was already well on the way toward a kind of sanctification as the greatest of American heroes. He was regarded as both the Great Union-Saver and the Great Emancipator. So it was quite complimentary to Stevens that, at his memorial services in the House of Representatives, a few of his eulogists saw fit to compare him with the late martyred president. "His name, with that of Lincoln," one of the speakers said, "will ever be remembered with the warmest emotions of gratitude by this and succeeding generations of the emancipated people of America, when others now esteemed great shall have been forgotten."

Time indeed has a way with reputations. Among the "emancipated people of America," Lincoln is no longer remembered with quite the same "emotions of gratitude" that he once was. Writing in a recent issue of *Ebony* magazine, a black historian, Lerone Bennett, Jr., raises the question "Was Abe Lincoln a White Supremacist?" Bennett answers in the affirmative, citing, among other evidence, a statement that Lincoln made in one of his debates with Stephen A. Douglas, at Charleston, Illinois, on September 18, 1858: "I . . . am not . . . in favor of bringing about in any way the social and political equality of the white and black races." In a book entitled *Black Power U.S.A.*, Bennett writes: "Lincoln grew during the war — but he didn't grow much. On every issue relating to the black man — on Emancipation, on the use and protection of black soldiers, on the confiscation and distribution of rebel property — he was vague, dilatory, contradictory." Stevens makes quite a contrast, in Bennett's view. Stevens "was the greatest parliamentary leader in American history. Even today, even after Kennedy and Lyndon Johnson, it is difficult to grasp the meaning of this strange, brilliant man who was the best friend black people have ever had in power."[1]

This preference for Stevens over Lincoln on the part of today's black leaders is both understandable and justifiable. Nevertheless, Lincoln still deserves his reputation as the Great Emancipator. He deserves it not so much because of the Emancipation Proclamation itself as because of the support he gave to the Thirteenth Amendment, which (unlike the Proclamation) definitely brought an end to chattel slavery throughout the land. True, he had been driven toward a more and more positive stand by the pressure of Stevens and other Radical Republicans. They, as much as he, deserve credit for the final emancipation. And, of course, emancipation had to come before the masses of black people could make any progress toward political and social equality.

If Lincoln lagged behind the Radicals, if they had to pull him along, it must be remembered that he, in his position, could not afford to be so far advanced or so singleminded. He had to hold the North together and direct the war effort so as to achieve a victory that would reunite the nation. He had to act as the president of the Conservatives as well as the Radicals, the Democrats as well as the Republicans, the Southerners as well as the Northerners. None of the Radicals represented any such broad constituency. Stevens, for one, had a very narrow power base; he was responsible only to the Republican majority within a small portion of a single state — the Lancaster district of Pennsylvania.

Suppose he and Lincoln had traded places. Alexander K. McClure, a Pennsylvanian who had been well acquainted with both men, speculated about this a generation later, in the 1890's. "I doubt not," McClure then wrote, "that Stevens, had he been in Lincoln's position, would have been greatly sobered by the responsibility that the President must accept for himself alone, and I doubt not that if Lincoln had been a Senator or Representative in Congress, he would have declared in favor of Emancipation long before he did it as President."

Stevens may be described as an agitator, Lincoln as a harmonizer. Both types are indispensable in our democratic system. Without the one, the system makes no advance. Without the other, it lacks stability. In their respective roles Stevens and Lincoln were among the ablest, if not the ablest, that this country has ever known. Not that either was simply the embodiment of an ideal; each had his human faults, and neither thought of himself as perfect. Stevens once said he pretended to no "prudish sanctity," and Lincoln asked to be painted as he was, "warts and all." It is naive to look for perfection in our political leaders, either past or present. It is a kind of naiveté that eventually sours and turns into a corroding cynicism.

Let us honor both Abraham Lincoln and Thaddeus Stevens for what they were. In honoring them we honor ourselves.

NOTE

1. Lerone Bennett, Jr., *Black Power U.S.A.: The Human Side of Reconstruction, 1867-1877* (Chicago: Johnson Publishing, 1967), pp. 15, 35.

⟦ VII ⟧

Lincoln, the Civil War,
and the American Mission

THE END of the Civil War was almost in sight when, on March 4, 1865, Abraham Lincoln delivered his second inaugural address. Looking back four years to the start of the conflict, he then said with reference to the Confederacy and the Union, Jefferson Davis and himself: "Both parties deprecated war; but one of them would *make* war rather than let the nation survive; and the other would *accept* war rather than let it perish. And the war came."[1]

Why had Lincoln been willing to take the risk of war? Why was he determined to save the Union even at the possible cost of horrendous bloodshed? Was there no other choice?

After Lincoln's election in November 1860, the nation faced a secession crisis. South Carolina took the first step on December 20, leading the way for the withdrawal of the rest of the states of the lower South. Congress and the Northern people discussed three possible courses for the federal government to follow.

One was, in the words of Horace Greeley, the influential editor of the *New York Tribune*, to "let the erring sisters go in peace,"

An address at a conference on Lincoln's thought and the present, Sangamon State University, Springfield, Illinois, June 11, 1976. Reprinted by permission from *The Public and the Private Lincoln: Contemporary Perspectives*, ed. Cullom Davis et al. (Carbondale: Southern Illinois University Press, 1979), pp. 137-46.

that is, to let the seceding states leave, and good riddance to them (though, in fact, Greeley did not intend to let them go unless they met certain fairly strict conditions that he prescribed). The second proposal was to find some compromise that would hold the states together. After all, there had been threats of disunion before, and the danger had been averted each time — by the Missouri Compromise, the compromise tariff of 1833, and the Compromise of 1850. Why not a compromise of 1860 now? The third possibility was, in the phrase of its advocates, to "enforce the laws" of the federal government. Though to its friends a simple matter of law and order, this seemed to its opponents like the "coercion" of sovereign states. The use of force against the states was, in the eyes of many Southerners, an evil to be resisted by force.[2]

The third of these choices was Lincoln's first, the one he favored from the outset. He was not making a deliberate decision for war, however, when he decided to provision Fort Sumter, to reinforce it if provisioning should be resisted, and in either case to make at least a show of maintaining the federal authority. We need not turn aside even to consider the old Confederate charge, repeated by Southern historians as recently as a generation ago, that Lincoln consciously and cleverly "maneuvered" the Confederates into firing the first shot so as to provoke a war that would save him, his party, and his country. The fact is that Jefferson Davis and the Confederates had already made their decision to capture the fort, and they would very soon have attacked it even if Lincoln had never thought of sending an expedition there. So much for the provocation charge. But it is quite a different thing to suggest that Lincoln considered the possibility, indeed the probability, of a conflict of arms resulting from his provisioning attempt. And it is not too much to say — for he said it himself — that he was determined to manage the project in such a way as to put the blame for war, if war should ensue, clearly and unmistakably upon the other side.[3]

As for compromise, Lincoln had never given it serious consideration. He did not pursue the idea of removing the garrison from

Fort Sumter in exchange for the adjournment of the Virginia secession convention, if indeed he ever really entertained the idea. He showed little enthusiasm for the work of the congressional committees on compromise, or for that of the Washington peace conference. True, he endorsed at least one of the constitutional amendments that Senator John J. Crittenden, of his own native Kentucky, proposed — the one to guarantee slavery forever in the states where it existed. But Lincoln rejected the key part of the Crittenden Compromise, that is, the proposal to run an east-west line through the territories and permit slavery below the line. To him, this plan was unacceptable on political grounds, the Republican platform having been built upon a Free-Soil plank which called for the complete exclusion of slavery from the territories. The Crittenden plan, as he viewed it, was also wrong in principle and would be a failure in practice. To allow slavery south of a particular line would only be to invite proslavery expansionists to annex all the territory they could to the south of it — in the Caribbean and in Central America. If it were to have a chance with the secessionists, any plan would have to concede, at the very least, the right of slavery to expand. To Lincoln, therefore, compromise did not seem like a real alternative.[4]

Nor did the other possibility — to "let the erring sisters go in peace," to accept disunion and learn to live with it. "Physically speaking, we cannot separate," Lincoln explained in his first inaugural. "We cannot remove our respective sections from each other, nor build an impassable wall between them." Inconceivable to Lincoln in 1861 was anything, on this continent, like the Berlin Wall of 1961 or the long strip of minefield and barbed wire that separates the two halves of divided Germany. "Suppose you go to war, you cannot fight always," Lincoln went on, addressing the disaffected people of the South, "and when, after much loss on both sides, and no gain on either, you cease fighting, the identical old questions, as to terms of intercourse, are again upon you."[5] What Lincoln really wanted, of course, was continued union together with continued peace.

Yet he was ready, if it should come to that, to sacrifice peace for the Union. "The only thing like passion or infatuation in the man," Walt Whitman was later to say of him, "was the passion for the Union of These States."[6] Not that Lincoln was an unthinking superpatriot, a mere chauvinist. He was a nationalist, to be sure, but one of a special, unselfish, idealistic sort. "He loved his country partly because it was his own country, but mostly because it was a free country; and he burned with a zeal for its advancement, prosperity and glory, because he saw in such, the advancement, prosperity and glory, of human liberty, human right, and human nature."[7] That is a quotation from Lincoln's eulogy of Henry Clay, but the words fit Lincoln himself equally well, or better. He, too, saw the cause of all humanity in the cause of the Union. America, the hope of the world!

This last conviction did not originate with either Clay or Lincoln. It had found expression much earlier, among statesmen and thinkers of the young Republic and even of the English colonies while they were new. Indeed, the idea goes back to the very discovery of America. It once applied to South America as well as North — to the whole of the Western hemisphere. The New World was to be a model for the Old. Such was the belief in the beginning.

Christopher Columbus started the great American Dream, the vision of a land of innocence as well as abundance, a land that by its very existence was a rebuke to Europe. On returning from his first voyage of discovery, in 1493, Columbus wrote the sovereigns of Spain a letter in which he described the New World's inhabitants as a carefree people who wore no clothes, had no weapons, fought no wars, laid claim to no private property, but lived on terms of perfect equality and, without having to work, received from a bounteous nature everything they needed.

This picture, elaborated by other travelers, had a revolutionary effect on European thought. It provoked a crisis of conscience. If there was somewhere a continent with human beings who enjoyed equality, peace, and general happiness, then what curse must have fallen upon Europe to account for so much misery and strife! Sir Thomas More commented upon the ills of contemporary England through the Utopia that he located in the New World. Jean Jacques Rousseau hailed the natural man of America as an exemplar for the poor European, the victim of a corrupting civilization. The image of pristine America helped to prepare the way for reform and revolution in Europe — and in America as well.[8]

Unlike Rousseau, the Puritans of New England saw evil in the wilderness, yet they too looked upon the New World as the home, at least prospectively, of the ideal society. The building of such a society as an example for all mankind was the task to which they set themselves. With God's cooperation they hoped to succeed, but they had a feeling that, succeed or fail, they were being watched. "For we must consider that we shall be as a City upon a hill," John Winthrop advised his fellow colonists in a sermon he wrote on shipboard approaching Massachusetts Bay in 1630. "The eyes of all people are upon us. So that if we shall deal falsely with our God in this work we have undertaken, and so cause him to withdraw his present help from us, we shall be made a story and a by-word throughout the world."[9] Descendants of the Puritans were to identify God's chosen people with the citizens of the United States.

The United States came into being supposedly as a delayed fulfillment of God's and nature's promise. Obviously the promise of the New World had not been realized before 1776, not in the English colonies at any rate, for the colonists had much to complain about. The fault must be the continuing and corrupting influence of the mother country; the cure, a complete separation from it. In the Declaration of Independence Thomas Jefferson wrote confidently of "self-evident" truths — "that all men are created equal, that they are endowed by their Creator with certain unalienable Rights, that among these are Life, Liberty, and the pursuit of Happiness." These propositions were by no means self-evident before the discovery of America. In presenting them Jefferson was echoing John Locke, but, consciously or not, he was also catching the distant echo of Christopher Columbus.

Those who believed the Revolutionary War was being fought for more than mere independence — and George Washington was one of them — did not feel that the Revolution ended with the war. General Washington doubtless expressed the aspirations of many when, in 1783, he sent a circular to the various states to announce the final victory and to urge the formation of a strong national government. He said:

> The Citizens of America, placed in the most enviable condition, as the sole lords and Proprietors of a vast Tract of Continent, comprehending all the various soils and climates of the World, and abounding with all the necessaries and conveniencies of life, are now by the late satisfactory pacification, acknowledged to be possessed of absolute freedom and independency. They are, from this period, to be considered as the Actors on a most conspicuous Theater, which seems to be peculiarly designated by Providence for the display of human greatness and felicity: Here, they are not only surrounded with every thing which can contribute to the completion of private and domestic enjoyment, but Heaven has crowned all its other blessings, by giving a fairer opportunity for political happiness, than any other Nation has ever been favored with. . . . The foundation of our Empire was not laid in the gloomy age of Ignorance and Superstition, but at an Epocha when the rights of mankind were better understood . . . than at any former period.

Washington went on to say that there was "an option still left to the United States of America." Its people could choose their own destiny. "This is the time of their political probation," he said in language reminiscent of Winthrop, "this is the moment when the eyes of the whole World are turned upon them, this is the moment to establish or ruin their national Character forever."

And in language anticipating Lincoln: "It is yet to be decided, whether the Revolution must ultimately be considered as a blessing or a curse: . . . not to the present age alone, for with our fate will the destiny of unborn Millions be involved."[10]

The Revolution found fulfillment in the Constitution of 1787.

Here was another instance of God's favor to the United States and another example to the rest of the world. So it seemed to President Washington, among others. In his Farewell Address, 1796, he imparted to his fellow citizens his hope "that Heaven may continue to you the choicest tokens of its beneficence . . . that the free constitution . . . may be sacredly maintained . . . that, in fine, the happiness of the people of these States, under the auspices of liberty, may be made complete, by so careful a preservation and so prudent a use of this blessing as will acquire to them the glory of recommending it to the applause, the affection, and adoption of every nation which is yet a stranger to it."

In the same address the president advised the people to keep the New World politically apart from the Old. "Why, by interweaving our destiny with that of any part of Europe, entangle our peace and prosperity in the toils of European Ambition, Rivalship, Interest, Humor, or Caprice?"[11] Underlying the young Republic's policy of diplomatic independence was the persisting belief in the degeneracy and hopelessness of Europe, the vigor and potentiality of America.

There was, of course, a difference between the theory of American virtue and the fact of American vice, a difference that European critics never tired of pointing out. The imperfections of the United States — the persistence of slavery, the rise of an aggressive, expansionist spirit — became more and more visible during the first half of the nineteenth century. Believers in the American Dream had to take an increasingly apologetic stand. Daniel Webster, along with many others, was ashamed of his country's role in pursuit of what some called its Manifest Destiny. "I have always wished," he said in criticizing the annexation of Texas, "that this country should exhibit to the nations of the earth the example of a great, rich, and powerful republic, which is not possessed by a spirit of aggrandizement. It is an example, I think, due from us to the world, in favor of the character of republican government."[12] In opposing the Mexican War he repeated his wish that "this country should exhibit to the world the example of a powerful republic, without greediness and hunger of empire." To Webster it seemed that democracy — or republicanism — could be spread much more successfully by the force of example than by the force of arms.

Lincoln, as one of Webster's fellow Whigs, also spoke out against the Mexican War. From the 1830's on he became more and more concerned about proslavery expansionism and proslavery lawlessness. After the mob killing of the Alton abolitionist Elijah Lovejoy he lectured to the young men of Springfield on the threat to the future of democracy. Lincoln and his contemporaries could hardly pretend that the democratic ideals of the Declaration of Independence had been brought even close to realization, but he was no less devoted to the ideals because of that. He came to look upon the United States as an experiment to see if the principles of the Declaration and the Constitution could be made to work. The experiment, he believed, was of vital interest not only to Americans but also to the whole "family of man," for the outcome would determine the future of self-government throughout the world.

Defenders of slavery began, in their desperateness, to repudiate the principles of the Declaration. In 1848 John C. Calhoun, the South Carolina nullificationist, denounced as "the most false and dangerous of all political errors" the proposition that "all men are born free and equal." Calhoun proceeded to aver: "Taking the proposition literally . . . there is not a word of truth in it. It begins with 'all men are born,' which is utterly untrue. Men are not born. Infants are born."[13] (Of course, the phrase in the Declaration actually reads "all men are *created*"; Calhoun's distortion of it shows how desperate he was for an argument.) He insisted that, if the Union should ever break up, the root cause of the catastrophe would be the propagation of the idea of human equality and freedom. (Here Calhoun was probably right.)

Lincoln deplored the propaganda of those who, as he put it, were "beginning to assail and to ridicule the white-man's charter of freedom — the declaration that 'all men are created free and equal.'" He commented: "This sounds strangely in republican

100

America. The like was not heard in the fresher days of the Republic."[14] Americans, some of them, were falling away from the great secular faith of their fathers.

The "white-man's charter of freedom," Lincoln had called it. What about the black man? Was not he, too, created free and equal? Was not the Declaration also the black man's charter? More and more, Lincoln by his own logic was driven in the direction of an affirmative answer. In 1854 he said: "When the white man governs himself that is self-government; but when he governs himself, and also governs *another* man, that is *more* than self-government — that is despotism. If the Negro is a *man,* why then my ancient faith teaches me that 'all men are created equal'; and that there can be no moral right in connection with one man's making a slave of another."[15] At that time Lincoln left unspoken the next conclusion to be drawn from the same logic, namely, that there could be no moral right in one man's making a social and political inferior of another merely because of race.

In 1858, however, Lincoln expounded the Declaration in such a way as to carry his reasoning much further. "I think the authors of that notable instrument intended to include *all* men," he said in one of his debates with Stephen A. Douglas, "but they did not intend to declare all men equal *in all respects.* . . . They defined with tolerable distinctness, in what respects they did consider all men created equal — equal in 'certain inalienable rights, among which are life, liberty, and the pursuit of happiness.' " The authors of the Declaration were quite aware of the fact that, in 1776, blacks did not enjoy full equality with whites, and whites did not enjoy full equality with one another. The authors did not pretend to be describing American society as it actually existed at that time. Lincoln continued: "They meant to set up a standard maxim for free society, which should be familiar to all, and revered by all; constantly looked to, constantly labored for, and even though never perfectly attained, constantly approximated, and thereby constantly spreading and deepening its influence, and augmenting the happiness and value of life to all people of all colors everywhere."[16]

To "all people of all colors everywhere"! Lincoln still saw the American ideal as an inspiration for the rest of the world. But it could be an effective inspiration for others only to the extent that Americans lived up to it themselves. Lincoln said he hated Douglas's attitude of indifference toward the spread of slavery into new territories. "I hate it because of the monstrous injustice of slavery itself," he explained. "I hate it because it deprives our republican example of its just influence in the world — enables the enemies of free institutions, with plausibility, to taunt us as hypocrites."[17] Lincoln condemned the antiforeigner, anti-Catholic Know-Nothing movement for much the same reason. "As a nation," he wrote,

> we began by declaring that *"all men are created equal."* We now practically read it "all men are created equal, *except Negroes.*" When the Know-Nothings get control, it will read "all men are created equal, except Negroes, *and foreigners, and catholics.*" When it comes to this I should prefer emigrating to some country where they make no pretence of loving liberty — to Russia, for instance, where despotism can be taken pure, and without the base alloy of hypocrisy.[18]

When the secession crisis arose in 1860, Lincoln felt that the United States was on trial before the world — much as Winthrop, more than two centuries earlier, had thought the colony of Massachusetts Bay on trial. After the coming of the Civil War, Lincoln developed and perfected an idea he had expressed as early as 1838. Referring to our revolutionary forefathers, he then had said: "Their ambition aspired to display before an admiring world, a practical demonstration of the truth of a proposition, which had hitherto been considered, at best no better, than problematical, namely, *the capability of a people to govern themselves.*" In his July 4, 1861, message to Congress, his first message after the fall of Fort Sumter, he declared that the issue between North and South involved more than the future of the United States. "It presents to the whole family of man, the question, whether a Constitutional republic, or a democracy — a government of the people, by the same people — can, or cannot, maintain its territorial integrity, against its own domestic foes." And finally at Gettysburg he made the culminating, the supreme statement, concluding with the familiar words: "that from these honored dead we take increased devotion to that cause for which they gave the last full measure of devotion — that we here highly resolve that these dead shall not have died in vain — that this nation, under God, shall have a new birth of freedom — and that government of the people, by the people, for the people, shall not perish from the earth."[19]

That is what the Civil War was about, as Lincoln saw it. That is what was at stake in 1860, in the threatened "destruction of our national fabric, with all its benefits, its memories, and its hopes," to quote again from the first inaugural address.[20] That is why Lincoln could not consent to a peaceful separation of the Union; why he could not agree to a compromise at the sacrifice of Free Soil; why he chose to make, at Fort Sumter, a symbolic Union-saving gesture that might lead, and did lead, to a Union-saving war.

At stake was a tradition that stretched back through the founding of the Republic to the discovery of America: from Abraham Lincoln to George Washington, Thomas Jefferson, John Winthrop, and on back to Christopher Columbus. It had become the secular religion of the American people. Some today might refer to it as the great American myth. Let those be cynical who will. There is something to be said for such a secular religion, even in our own time, especially in our own time. It would not be altogether bad if American leaders still believed and still acted on the belief that the United States had a special calling — not a Manifest Destiny to expand and to conquer, but a sacred mission to set an example for the rest of the world by living up to its own historic ideals.

NOTES

1. Roy P. Basler, Marion Dolores Pratt, and Lloyd A. Dunlap, eds., *The Collected Works of Abraham Lincoln* (New Brunswick, N.J.: Rutgers, University Press, 1953-55), 8:332.

2. See Kenneth M. Stampp, *And the War Came: The North and the*

Secession Crisis, 1860-1861 (Baton Rouge: Louisiana State University Press, 1950), pp. 31-45.

3. The most scholarly statement of the case against Lincoln is Charles W. Ramsdell, "Lincoln and Fort Sumter," *Journal of Southern History* 3 (August 1937): 259-88. For a defense of Lincoln, see Richard N. Current, "The Confederates and the First Shot," *Civil War History* 7 (December 1961): 357-69, also reprinted in this volume. Lincoln explained in his July 4, 1861, message to Congress: "The Executive . . . having said to them [the seceders] in the inaugural address, 'You can have no conflict without being yourselves the aggressors,' . . . took pains, not only to keep this declaration good, but also to keep the case so free from the power of ingenious sophistry as that the world should not be able to misunderstand it" (Lincoln, *Collected Works*, 4:425).

4. See especially Lincoln to Thurlow Weed, December 17, 1860, in Lincoln, *Collected Works*, 4:154. On the question of evacuating Fort Sumter, see Richard N. Current, *Lincoln and the First Shot* (Philadelphia: Lippincott, 1963), pp. 92-96.

5. Lincoln, *Collected Works*, 4:259.

6. Allen T. Rice, ed., *Reminiscences of Abraham Lincoln by Distinguished Men of His Time* (New York: North American, 1886), p. 475.

7. Lincoln, *Collected Works*, 2:126.

8. See Arturo Uslar Peitri, "Eso que los Europeos Llamaron Nuevo Mundo," *Américas* 28 (April 1976): 9-16.

9. Robert C. Winthrop, *Life and Letters of John Winthrop* (Boston: Ticknor and Fields, 1867), p. 19.

10. John C. Fitzpatrick, ed., *The Writings of George Washington: From the Original Manuscript Sources, 1745-1799* (Washington: Government Printing Office, 1931-44), 26:483-86.

11. Ibid., 35:217-18, 234.

12. Daniel Webster. *The Works of Daniel Webster* (Boston: Little, Brown, 1855), 5:56, 288.

13. Richard K. Cralle, ed., *The Works of John C. Calhoun* (New York: D. Appleton, 1851-57), 4:507.

14. Lincoln, *Collected Works*, 2:130-31.

15. Ibid., p. 266.

16. Lincoln made this statement in his Springfield speech of June 26, 1857, and repeated it in his Alton debate with Douglas, October 15, 1858. Ibid., pp. 405-6; 3:301.

17. Ibid., 2:255; repeated 3:14.

18. Ibid., 2:323.

19. Ibid., 1:113, 4:426, 7:23.

20. Ibid., 4:266.

⟦ VIII ⟧

Unity, Ethnicity,
and Abraham Lincoln

"GETTING RIGHT with Lincoln" used to be a ritual among
Americans of widely differing persuasions.[1] Republican
politicans tried to show, especially each February 12, that Lincoln
if alive would agree with them. Not only Republicans but also
Democrats sought his implied endorsement. So, too, did many
others — conservatives and Communists, atheists and spiritual-
ists, black advocates and white supremacists, nativists and immigrants. All did obeisance to the memory of Lincoln; all claimed
his spirit as their own. Many, of course, still do.

In recent years, however, increasing numbers of Americans have
turned away from Lincoln. Conspicuous among them are the
blacks. Though some of the older blacks continue to honor him
as the Great Emancipator, most of the younger ones seem to have
repudiated him as a racist and a colonizationist.[2] Less noticed —
and hence more in need of attention — is the tendency toward
disaffection among the "white ethnics," the Americans of comparatively recent Eastern and Southern European stock. Though

First annual R. Gerald McMurtry Lecture, Louis A. Warren Lincoln Library and
Museum, Fort Wayne, Indiana, May 11, 1978. Reprinted by permission from
Richard N. Current, *Unity, Ethnicity, & Abraham Lincoln* (Fort Wayne: Warren
Lincoln Library and Museum, 1978).

many of the newer immigants and their descendants no doubt continue to admire Lincoln, the leaders of the "new ethnicity" movement do not consider him vital or even relevant to their cause.

"Now he belongs to the ages," Edwin M. Stanton is supposed to have remarked at Lincoln's deathbed. So far as the majority of blacks are concerned, that might be rephrased to read today: "Now he belongs only to honkies." If the advocates of the new ethnicity should have their way, the statement might soon need to be further revised, so as to read: "Now he belongs only to WASPs."

[1]

At one time the name and fame of Lincoln held great significance for America's immigrants. That was the case during the first three decades of the present century, when immigration and assimilation were leading topics of controversy in the United States.

In the early 1900's the numbers of foreigners annually arriving in this country set new records year after year — almost a million and a quarter in 1905. A larger and larger proportion came not from the earlier sources, not from Great Britain, Germany, and the Scandinavian countries, but from the countries of Eastern and Southern Europe, which provided nearly three-fourths of the total arriving between 1900 and 1910.

Among the Americans whose ancestors had arrived earlier, some looked upon the newcomers as largely inferior peoples who ought to be carefully screened or entirely excluded. Some thought that, at the very least, care should be taken to see that these strangers to American ways were properly Americanized. Others continued to rely on the "melting pot," confident that the newer elements would blend in, as the older ones presumably had done, and that the better qualities of each would be added to the amalgam of a constantly improving American people and American civilization. Still others, much the fewest of all, preferred to keep the different nationalities more or less distinct and to preserve in the United States a great variety of harmoniously coexisting groups and cultures.[3]

106

World War I temporarily checked the influx of immigrants, but not the debate about them. Once the United States had entered the war, the strains grew more intense than ever, as the Old World ties of British-Americans, German-Americans, Irish-Americans, and other "hyphenated" Americans came into conflict. In response to postwar xenophobia, Congress passed the immigration restriction acts of 1921 and 1924, which discriminated against the more recently arriving nationalities. No longer was immigration itself a serious "problem," but there remained the question of what to do about the already present immigrants and their children.

Throughout the controversy the name of Lincoln had often been seen and heard. Advocates of strict Americanization, of melting-pot assimilation, and of preserving immigrant inheritances — but seldom if ever the advocates of exclusion — appealed to his memory for support. Immigrants themselves accepted him as a favorite hero.

Generally the older-stock immigrants and their descendants needed little or no indoctrination. Germans and Scandinavians could boast, though the evidence was hardly conclusive, that their forefathers had managed to get right with Lincoln long ago and, indeed, had been responsible for his election in 1860. Some German-Americans even claimed Lincoln as one of them — a German — on the basis of an old Land Office warrant made out to his grandfather Abraham *Linkhorn,* a perfectly good Germanic name.[4]

The Americanization programs of the period were directed primarily to the immigrants of the more recent national origins. These programs had an important place in the activities of the settlement houses, in special night courses to prepare adults for naturalization, and above all in the curriculum of the public schools.

One of the teacher guides, titled *A Course in Patriotism and Citizenship,* published in 1914 and republished in 1918, referring to the ideals of the Pilgrims, the Revolutionary leaders, and Lincoln, declared: "These ideals must become the heritage not only of every American-born child, but of every alien as well." The book mentioned Lincoln more often than any other historical figure, even George Washington. In classroom plans for the first grade through the sixth, the teacher could find advice on using Lincoln as a model. Selected incidents from his life would show he "had a heart brimful of kindness," pitied the poor black slaves and "caused them to be freed," "was always good to his mother," constantly tried to improve himself by study, and was a great statesman because he loved "his *whole* country" and fostered "good will among all citizens." In short, he embodied the American spirit — "courage in the face of difficulties, loyalty to truth, sympathy and courtesy, industry and reverence to God and to one's fellowmen."[5]

Such was the Lincoln theme as it was utilized by the strict Americanizationists, by those who viewed assimilation as a one-way process through which the newcomers and their descendants would be compelled to give up their European inheritance and adopt American ways. But Lincoln also served the purposes of assimilationists who saw the melting pot as a mutual and voluntary process to which the Europeans also had a positive contribution to make.

One of these assimilationists was Emory S. Bogardus, a social scientist of Dutch colonial ancestry who in Chicago in 1908 had begun "to teach the English language and American principles to the foreign-born," especially the Poles. Largely on the basis of that experience Bogardus wrote a book, *Essentials of Americanization,* which went through three editions in 1919, 1920, and 1923. To Bogardus, forced Americanization was as bad as forced Prussianization or Russianization. Lincoln therefore was especially relevant to him, for Lincoln had subordinated nationalism to individualism. With Lincoln, "the appeal was to the Union, not as an end for purposes of national glorification; but for safeguarding the liberties of the individual, and for the widest, most consistent expression of personality." Lincoln was a symbol not only of democracy and justice but also of individual opportunity — a man who "rose from the depths of poverty and obscurity to the heights of fame and service." He had been, and still was, definitely on the side of the poor immigrant. "The employer needs to realize," Bogardus wrote, "that labor, as Abraham Lincoln said, takes precedence over capital in industrial enterprises. The welfare of labor, even un-skilled immigrant labor, is a more important factor than the welfare of capital."[6]

Also citing Lincoln was a social scientist with yet another back-ground and point of view — Julius Drachsler, a young assistant professor at Smith College, a Jew of Czechoslovakian birth. In 1920 Drachsler proposed the experiment of "consciously creating a composite culture in America." This would be done by "deliber-ately furthering an interest in the cultural achievements of the im-migrant groups and by systematically bringing before the minds of their descendants these variegated culture-materials." It would be a cooperative undertaking, private and public. For the various groups, "voluntary cultural organizations" would conserve the "unique values of their heritage." The state would "find its proper function in the harmonization of these values, through a synthetic cultural curriculum in its public educational system."

All this would require a conception of democracy — "cultural democracy" — that was quite different from the "common no-tion of Americanization." Fortunately, the "popular imagination" already was close to grasping the "kernel" of this idea. "To the American mind," Drachsler explained, ". . . Abraham Lincoln is the embodiment of Democratic personality. His freedom in min-gling with men of all sorts, his simplicity, almost crudity of man-ners, his surpassing warmth and human sympathy, his just treat-ment of high and low alike, are the qualities of his character on which the people's fancy loves to linger." And these were the qual-ities of cultural democracy.[7]

Proponents of restricting immigration — of "closing the gates" — showed little enthusiasm for the use that others were making of the Lincoln image. One of the most prestigious of the restrictionists was Edward Alsworth Ross, professor of sociology at the University of Wisconsin. In the preface to his book *The Old*

World in the New (1914) Ross wrote: " 'Immigration,' said to me a distinguished social worker and idealist, 'is a wind that blows democratic ideas throughout the world. In a Siberian hut from which four sons had gone forth to America to seek their fortune, I saw tacked up a portrait of Lincoln cut from a New York newspaper. Even there they knew what Lincoln stood for and loved him.' " What he stood for, according to the "idealist" whom Ross was quoting, were "American ideas of freedom and opportunity." Ross went on to express his own fear, which formed the thesis of his book, that the United States would soon cease to be a land of democracy, of freedom and opportunity, if it should continue to be overrun by the new barbarian hordes.[8]

Not only were those immigrants from Siberia enthusiastic, but so were immigrants from many other parts of the world. Mary Antin, who a couple of decades earlier had arrived as a Jewish girl from Russia, noted in *The Promised Land* (1912) "how many 'green' pupils entered school last September, not knowing the days of the week in English, who next February will be declaiming patriotic verses in honor of George Washington and Abraham Lincoln, with a foreign accent, indeed, but with plenty of enthusiasm."[9]

Mary Antin herself admired Washington the most, but the favorite of the great majority of the immigrants was Lincoln. "Far more than any other American, Lincoln makes the immigrants feel that this is their country as well as the country of the native-born," a free-lance writer, Grace Humphrey, declared in 1917. "So they have adopted him for their own, perhaps because they share with him the pioneer spirit; they, too, have adventured into a new country where life is difficult and hardships many. Like him, they have struggled with unfavorable surroundings, against ignorance and extreme poverty." Ms. Humphrey proceeded to give touching examples of Lincoln devotees who in origin were Russian, Lithuanian, Polish, Italian, or Hungarian, several of them Jews. "And to native-born Americans," she concluded, "the immigrants' love of Lincoln suggests a kindling of our patriotism, a new dedication

110

of ourselves to the things for which he lived and died, to the Lincoln ideal, the truest symbol of American democracy."[10]

[2]

Americans of diverse national backgrounds continued for some time to honor Lincoln and the values be symbolizes, such as personal liberty, individual opportunity, and national union. President Franklin D. Roosevelt made him an honorary sponsor first of the New Deal and then of the anti-Axis war effort.[11] World War II had no such traumatic effect on ethnic relations in the United States as World War I had had. During the 1940's representatives of various nationality groups cooperated on the Common Council for American Unity to encourage assimilation of the true melting-pot kind. The Council published *Common Ground.* "Never has it been more important," the magazine averred, "that we become intelligently aware of the ground Americans of various strains have in common . . . that we reawaken the old American Dream, the dream which, in its powerful emphasis on the fundamental worth and dignity of every human being, can be a bond of unity no totalitarian attack can break."[12]

During the postwar decades of booming prosperity, the once largely impecunious ethnic groups seemed rapidly to be realizing the American Dream, at least insofar as that dream promised a chance for everyone to rise in the world. One researcher, the Reverend Andrew Greeley, a Roman Catholic of Irish extraction, produced some rather startling evidence in this regard. From responses to questionnaires between 1963 and 1974, Greeley made the following deductions: his own group, the Irish Catholic, was the "best educated Gentile group in American society," and the Italian and Polish Catholics were making the most rapid educational rise. Next to the Jews, the Irish Catholics also enjoyed the highest family income. After these two groups stood, in descending order, the Italian, the German, and the Polish Catholics; then the Episcopalians and other Protestants of various denominations;

and, at the very bottom, the Baptists. Though, as Greeley himself recognized, there were "limitations in the data" available to him, there seems little reason to doubt his basic conclusions: "The Jewish immigrants clearly have become immensely successful," and "considerable numbers of Catholics have 'made it' into the middle class and this must be counted, at least to some extent, a success for the American political, social, and economic experiment."[13]

Nevertheless, Greeley joined with a few other Catholic and a few Jewish intellectuals to renounce the American Dream as an illusion and to promote in its place a great variety of ideals, a different set of them for each ethnic group. Prominent among the disaffected intellectuals, in addition to Greeley, were Monsignor Geno Baroni, son of an Italian coalminer in Pennsylvania; Michael Novak, mainly of Slovakian background; and Irving Levine, a Jew of Polish and Lithuanian descent. As another member of the "coterie" recalled, "a small coterie of about twenty people gave birth to what was called the 'ethnic movement.' "[14] These "white ethnics" imitated the Black Power movement, as the Indians and the Spanish-speaking minorities previously had done. If Americans with African, aboriginal, Mexican, or Puerto Rican ancestors received special consideration, why should not Americans with Eastern or Southern European ancestors obtain the same kind of preferential treatment?

A classic exposition of the new ethnicity is to be found in Michael Novak's book *The Rise of the Unmeltable Ethnics* (1972). According to Novak, the melting pot would not work — and should not work — in the case of his fellow Slovak-Americans. "The view that we shall become one by becoming *like* each other, more 'Americanized,' is really not an enlightened view," he maintains. To him the villains in the American drama are the Protestants of British ancestry, that is, the so-called White Anglo-Saxon Protestants, the WASPs. "The recent rise in ethnic assertion is due in large measure to the discrediting of traditional WASP styles," he says. The White Non-Anglo-Saxon Catholics (as they might conversely be called) have "acceded far too long to the pressure

112

of Americanization — which was really WASPification." Novak resents the kind of instruction he himself received in public school. "Nowhere in my schooling do I recall any attempt to put me in touch with my own history," he complains. "The strategy was to make an American of me."[15] Obviously this missionary of ethnicity and Catholicity does not look upon the Lincoln story as, in any sense, a part of his own historical background.

What Novak and the others denounce as "Americanization" they might more accurately refer to as "industrialization" or "modernization." It is a worldwide trend, though, to be sure, it has gone the farthest in the United States. The broad and ineluctable sweep of events — far more than the narrow kind of Americanization that nativists once tried to impose — has given shape to the middle-class culture that now predominates among Americans, whatever their national origin. Against the new cosmopolitanism there has risen a reaction, also worldwide, that may be termed the new tribalism. It takes the form of Quebeçois separatism in Canada, Scottish and Welsh nationalism in the United Kingdom, and other divisive movements in Europe, Asia, and Africa. It takes the form of a heightening ethnic self-consciousness and ethnic exclusiveness in the United States. What Novak and others like him really object to is the growing universalism of the twentieth century. What they are actually calling for is a return to the imaginary virtues of nineteenth-century European peasant life.

Instead of the term "new tribalism," the ethnicity advocates use the term "cultural pluralism" to describe their program. "Cultural pluralism" has an attractive sound largely because of its ambiguity. To many Americans it implies an appreciation for diverse folkways as ingredients of, or as supplements to, the prevailing American mixture. In that sense it is perfectly consistent with the melting-pot ideal. To the self-appointed ethnic spokesmen, however, it means the intensification of cultural differences as a means of maintaining group separateness.

In the name of "cultural pluralism" the ethnic agitators have undertaken to revolutionize American public education, and they have made considerable headway. Unlike Julius Drachsler, with his "cultural democracy" back in 1920, they would not leave the promotion and preservation of Old World cultures to private organizations but would force it on the public schools. The Ford and Rockefeller foundations have provided generous grants for the cause. The federal government is giving moral and monetary support in accordance with the Ethnic Heritage Studies Programs Act of 1972, which calls for the training of teachers to "teach the importance of ethnicity" and for "the rewriting of American history as ethnic history."[16] The educational establishment has added its approval, and pedagogical experts are busy refashioning the curriculum so as to emphasize ethnic studies.[17] A brand-new bibliography for schools lists materials on forty-four "ethnic groups" — from "American Indians" and "Appalachian Americans" to "Ukrainian Americans" and "Welsh Americans."[18]

A few sociologists and educators have raised doubts about the direction that "cultural pluralism" is taking. One of them points out that "in the schools we are still engaged, and must continue to be, in the making of Americans, since this is still a country of mass immigration with large populations still imperfectly integrated into a common nation."[19] In fact, the number of immigrants legally entering this country now runs to nearly 400,000 a year — much fewer than the million or more of the early 1900's, but still a sizable figure. Immigration currently accounts for about 20 percent of the country's population growth. The present immigration law, in effect since 1965, is far less restrictive than the laws of the 1920's, and it does not discriminate against people from Eastern or Southern Europe or from any other part of the world.

The new ethnic curriculum has little or no place for Abraham Lincoln. "To endorse cultural pluralism" the American Association of Colleges for Teacher Education has resolved, "is to endorse the principle that there is no one model American."[20] White ethnics naturally expect to celebrate their particular folk heroes while reviving and cherishing their separate folk cultures. Novak concedes "it is important that all students learn something of the

114

formative experiences of the nation" — including Washington, the Revolution, Lincoln, the Civil War, and all that.[21] For Novak and others like him, however, the nearest thing to one model American is no longer Lincoln. It is John F. Kennedy. When Protestants "talk about 'the old values,' " Novak says, ". . . they do not mean what southern and eastern European Catholics mean. The latter mean by morality a kind of inner placidity, easygoingness, carefreeness, a tough view of authority, even a bit of mischief (like Jack Kennedy, with has brashness and Irish ruthlessness)."[22] Nowadays the houses of white ethnics are frequently adorned with pictures or statuettes of Kennedy, not Lincoln.[23]

[3]

Lincoln in his own time was by no means a favorite among Catholic immigrants, and few if any of them would have displayed his portrait while he was still alive. They were almost all Democrats; he was a Whig and then a Republican, in either case a member of a party that had a reputation for nativism. Yet he was never a nativist himself. Indeed, his record as a political leader — his record on immigration and immigrants as well as on other matters — amply justifies the high significance he held, temporarily at least, for later Americans of every religion and every national origin.

When, in 1844, news came to Springfield, Illinois, of an anti-foreigner and anti-Catholic riot in Philadelphia, Lincoln called a public meeting to condemn the action of the Philadelphia mob and to deny the charge that the Whig party was to blame for it. He introduced resolutions, which the assembled Springfielders approved, to the effect that every immigrant should be admitted to citizenship as soon as he had been "put to some reasonable test of his fidelity to our country and its institutions" and had dwelled "among us a reasonable time to become generally acquainted with the nature of those institutions." Lincoln's resolutions stressed that "the guarantee of the rights of conscience, as found in our Constitution, is most sacred and inviolable, and one that belongs no

115

less to the Catholic than to the Protestant." Even the Democratic party newspaper of Springfield acknowledged Lincoln's personal sincerity. The Democratic editor commented: "Mr. Lincoln expressed the kindest and most benevolent feelings towards foreigners; they were, I doubt not, the sincere and honest sentiments of *his heart;* but they were not those of *his party.*"[24]

The Whigs and the Democrats were, of course, competing for the foreign vote. While doing so, both tried to attract and hold the support of the American born. The dilemma became especially acute for Lincoln in the 1850's when, as a Free-Soiler and an incipient Republican, he faced the challenge of the rising Know-Nothing party, with its demand for limiting the political rights of the foreign born in general and the Catholics in particular. He did not want to antagonize the Know-Nothings, for he hoped to win them over to the cause of resisting the extension of slavery. Yet he detested their prejudice, and he made his feelings known to everyone who inquired. He was supremely eloquent in a letter of August 24, 1855, to his friend Joshua Speed:

> I am not a Know-Nothing. That is certain. How could I be? How can any one who abhors the oppression of negroes be in favor of degrading classes of white people? Our progress in degeneracy appears to me to be pretty rapid. As a nation, we began by declaring that *"all men are created equal."* We now practically read it "all men are created equal, *except Negroes."* When the Know-Nothings get control, it will read "all men are created equal, except Negroes, *and foreigners, and catholics."* When it comes to this, I should prefer emigrating to some country where they make no pretence of loving liberty — to Russia, for instance, where despotism can be taken pure, without the base alloy of hypocrisy.

Far from being a nativist in his own thought and feeling, Lincoln maintained that the newly arrived immigrant could become as good an American as any native, even one with colonial ancestry. It was, in his view, a matter of belief, not birth. A person was an American by virtue of his commitment to American ideals. As Lincoln said at an Independence Day celebration in Chicago in July 1858:

116

We find a race of men living in that day [1776] whom we claim as our fathers and grandfathers; they were iron men, they fought for the principle that they were contending for; and we understand that by what they then did it has followed that the degree of prosperity that we now enjoy has come to us. We hold this annual celebration to remind ourselves of all the good done in this process of time, of how it was done and who did it, and how we are historically connected with it; and we go from these meetings in better humor with ourselves — we feel more attached the one to the other, and more firmly bound to the country we inhabit. In every way we are better men in the age, and race, and country in which we live for these celebrations. But after we have done all this we have not yet reached the whole. There is something else connected with it. We have besides these men — descended by blood from our ancestors — among us perhaps half our people who are not descendants at all of these men, they are men who have come from Europe — German, Irish, French and Scandinavian — men that have come from Europe themselves, or whose ancestors have come hither and settled here, finding themselves our equals in all things. If they look back through this history to trace their connection with those days by blood, they find they have none, they cannot carry themselves back into that glorious epoch and make themselves feel that they are part of us, but when they look through that old Declaration of Independence they find that those old men say that "We hold these truths to be self-evident, that all men are created equal," and then they feel that the moral sentiment taught in that day evidences their relation to those men, that it is the father of all moral principle in them, and that they have a right to claim it as though they were blood of the blood, and flesh of the flesh of the men who wrote that Declaration [loud and long continued applause], and so they are. That is the electric cord in that Declaration that links the hearts of patriotic and liberty-loving men together, that will link those patriotic hearts as long as the love of freedom exists in the minds of men throughout the world. [Applause.][25]

Eventually, almost all the Know-Nothings in the North joined the Republican party. Almost none of the Catholic immigrants did so. They were repelled by the new party's various isms — not only its nativism but also its sabbatarianism, prohibitionism, and abolitionism. Few if any of these people voted for Lincoln in 1860. He did garner the votes, however, of many of the Protestant immigrants, German and Scandinavian as well as British. He seemed to feel that he owed his election largely to such German politicians as Gustave Koerner of Illinois and Carl Schurz of Wisconsin, and he rewarded them generously with patronage.[26]

Yet Lincoln continued to favor free immigration for all, including the Germans and Irish who habitually voted Democratic. Speaking in Cincinnati on his way to Washington as president-elect in February 1861, he said: "In regard to Germans and [other] foreigners, I esteem foreigners no better than other people, and no worse." The United States, he went on, is "comparatively a new country," a land of opportunity, "and if they can better their condition by leaving their old homes, there is nothing in my heart to forbid them coming and I bid them all God speed."[27]

After the firing on Fort Sumter, most of the anti-Lincoln Democrats, the European born as well as the American born, had little enthusiasm for Mr. Lincoln's war, and they lost what little they had when he put the draft into effect and proclaimed emancipation as a war aim. Strong disapproval came, for example, from the Milwaukee *Seebote,* a German-language newspaper that served as the semi-official organ of Wisconsin's Catholic hierarchy. The *Seebote* expressed horror that European immigrants should be "used as fodder for cannons" in an abolitionist war; that, under Lincoln's proclamation, the "Germans, and Irish must be annihilated, to make room for the Negro."[28] Germans, Irishmen, Belgians, and Luxembourgers in Wisconsin rioted against the draft. An Irish mob in New York City demonstrated against both conscription and emancipation by killing hundreds of blacks.[29]

Draft resistance and draft evasion were among the numerous wartime concerns of Lincoln. So many men of foreign birth claimed exemption as aliens that, on May 8, 1863, he issued a proclamation on that subject. He announced he would accept no "plea of alienage" from any immigrant who had ever voted, and he would accept no such plea from any who had not voted but had declared an intention of becoming a citizen and was still in this country sixty-five days after the proclamation's date. Seven months afterward Lincoln reported to Congress: "There is reason to believe that many persons born in foreign countries, who have declared their intention to become citizens, or who have been fully naturalized, have evaded the military duty required of them by denying the fact."[30]

Lincoln still welcomed foreigners to the United States, even though he had, in effect, suggested that certain ones leave the country. Immigrants could come and remain without fear of the draft so long as they took no step toward naturalization and refrained from exercising one of the rights of citizenship, the right to vote. During the first three years of the war the immigration figures had been quite low in comparison with the prewar peak, and employers began to complain of a labor shortage. So Lincoln in December 1863 urged Congress to do something to encourage immigration, and Congress responded with the act of July 4, 1864, which authorized employers to bring in foreign workers under contract and deduct the cost of transportation from future wages.

In December 1864 Lincoln suggested that Congress amend the law so as to "prevent frauds against the immigrants while on their way and on their arrival." He also said: "I regard our emigrants [immigrants] as one of the principal replenishing streams which are appointed by Providence to repair the ravages of internal war and its wastes of national strength and health. All that is necessary is to secure the flow of that stream in its present fullness, and to that end the government must, in every way, make it manifest that it neither needs nor designs to impose involuntary military service upon those who come from other lands to cast their lot in our country."

Thus, both before and during his presidency, Lincoln set an example of hospitality and tolerance toward immigrants of whatever country, culture, or creed. He invited them to share not only in economic opportunity but also in the great political experiment that he considered the United States to be. Only time, he believed, would tell whether the principles of the Constitution and the Declaration of Independence would permanently work. The founders of the republic — in declaring that "all men are created equal" and are endowed with the rights of "life, liberty, and the pursuit of happiness" — intended to set up a "standard maxim for free society" to be "constantly labored for" and thereby to be constantly "augmenting the happiness and value of life to all people of all colors everywhere." The experiment, therefore, was of vital interest to the whole "family of man."[31]

[4]

The principles of the Declaration and the Constitution were in their ultimate origin as English as the men who proclaimed them, as English as the language the men used. The principles and the language have persisted, and along with them the predominance of the English tone in American civilization, mainly because the English were much the most numerous among those who originally settled. In no other country have so many different peoples come and managed to live together so successfully. They have managed it because, on the whole, they have accepted a common core of political values — the values that Lincoln so magnificently exemplified and so eloquently expressed. Yet educators of the present complain of "Anglo-conformity" and propose to teach American children that all ethnic heritages and all political traditions are of equal worth and relevance for life in the United States.

The hope that has drawn so many to this country — the hope for a new life in a new land — is at least as old as the discovery of America. And the vision of a new people emerging — one from many — is at least as old as the founding of the republic. At the end of the Revolutionary War this vision moved the pen of Michel de Crèvecoeur, a native of France, a resident of New York. "What then is the American, this new man?" Crèvecoeur inquired in his *Letters from an American Farmer* (1782). He went on to answer:

He is either an European, or the descendant of an European, hence that strange mixture of blood, which you will find in no other country. . . . *He* is an American who, leaving behind him all his ancient prejudices and manners, receives new ones from the new mode of life he has embraced, the new government he obeys, and the new rank he holds. . . . Here individuals of all nations are melted into a new race of men, whose labours and posterity will one day cause great changes in the world.[32]

True, the promise of American life is still in the process of fulfillment, as it has been for so long. It has not yet been and perhaps may never be perfectly realized. Still, as Lincoln once asked in regard to the American experiment, "Is there any better, or equal, hope in the world?" That is a good question for those who today would shatter the American dream and idealize its fragments — the separate Polish, Italian, Irish, Greek, Slovak, Hungarian, and dozens of other tribalistic dreams. They would do well to recall, too, another of Lincoln's admonitions: "A house divided against itself cannot stand."[33]

NOTES

1. See David Donald, "Getting Right with Lincoln," *Harper's Magazine* 202 (April 1951): 74-80; reprinted in Donald, *Lincoln Reconsidered* (New York: Knopf, 1966), pp. 3-18.

2. See Lerone Bennett, Jr., "Was Abe Lincoln a White Supremacist?" *Ebony* 23 (February 1968): 35-42. See also Mark E. Neely, Jr., "Emancipation: 113 Years Later," *Lincoln Lore* (Bulletin of the Lincoln National Life Foundation, Fort Wayne, Indiana) no. 1653 (November 1975). The Neely article summarizes and interprets the findings of Yvette Fulcher, who, as a student of Gabor S. Boritt's, made a survey of opinion on Lincoln among present-day blacks.

3. The term "melting pot" meant different things to different people in the early 1900's, as it does today. To some it has connoted the casting off of non-English elements as so much slag. In this sense it was repudiated by Horace M. Kallen, "Democracy versus the Melting-Pot," *Nation* 100 (February 18, 25, 1915): 190-94, 217-20; and by Randolph Bourne, "Trans-National America," *Atlantic Monthly* 118 (July 1916): 86-97. Kallen proposed a "democracy of nationalities" in the United States, a "harmony" instead of a "unison" of cultures, but he conceded that "the old Anglo-Saxon theme 'America' " should be "dominant, per-

haps, among others, but one among many" themes (pp. 219-20). Bourne thought the wartime revival of immigrant nationalisms had proved the melting pot a failure, but he favored a new cosmopolitan "integration" of American society to create a new "trans-nationality." As compared with Kallen's metaphor of the symphony, he preferred the image of a "weaving . . . of many threads of all sizes and colors," but he cautioned: "It would be folly to absorb the nations faster than we could weave them" (p. 96). In its true, historic meaning, the "melting" ideal may be viewed as essentially consistent with Kallen's "symphony" ideal and Bourne's "weaving" ideal. For an early (1782) statement of the "melting" principle, see the quotation, later in this chapter, from Michel de Crèvecoeur.

4. George M. Stephenson, *A History of American Immigration, 1820-1924* (Boston: Ginn, 1926), p. 132; Richard O'Connor, *The German-Americans: An Informal History* (Boston: Little, Brown, 1968), pp. 132-36; Albert B. Faust, *The German Element in the United States* (Boston: Houghton Mifflin, 1909), 2:183-84n. In *The Americanization of Edward Bok: The Autobiography of a Dutch Boy Fifty Years After* (New York: Scribner's, 1922), the highly successful magazine publisher concluded (pp. 451-52) with the hope that his adopted country might yet live up to its own ideals. "And I ask no greater privilege," Bok wrote, "than to be allowed to live to see my potential America become actual: the America that I like to think of as the America of Abraham Lincoln and of Theodore Roosevelt — not faultless, but less faulty."

5. Ella Lyman Cabot et al., *A Course in Patriotism and Citizenship* (Boston: Houghton Mifflin, 1914, 1918), pp. 169-70, 198, 210-11, 231, 242. See also Winthrop Talbot and Julia E. Johnson, eds., *Americanization: Principles of Americanism, Essentials of Americanization, Technic of Race-Assimilation, Annotated Bibliography* (New York: H. W. Wilson, 1920), pp. 23, 372-73.

6. Emory S. Bogardus, *Essentials of Americanization* (Los Angeles: University of Southern California Press, 1923), pp. 9, 57, 66-67, 80, 288.

7. Julius Drachsler, *Democracy and Assimilation: The Blending of Immigrant Heritages in America* (New York: Macmillan, 1920), pp. 184, 187, 211-13, 237. Drachsler was an assimilationist, as the title of his book indicates. He provided statistics (e.g., pp. 108, 149) to show the rapidly increasing intermarriage of different nationalities in New York City. What he favored was, essentially, a planned and improved functioning of the melting pot. This is close to what his contemporaries Kallen and Bourne advocated (see note 3, above).

8. Edward Alsworth Ross, *The Old World in the New: The Significance of the Past and Present Immigration to the American People* (New York: Century, 1914), preface. Kallen (see note 3, above) was responding to Ross.

9. Mary Antin, *The Promised Land* (Boston: Houghton Mifflin, 1912), p. 206.

10. Grace Humphrey, "Lincoln and the Immigrant," *Outlook* 115 (February 7, 1917): 234.

11. See Alfred H. Jones, *Roosevelt's Image Brokers: Poets, Playwrights, and the Use of the Lincoln Symbol* (Port Washington, N.Y.: Kennikat, 1974), pp. 43-47, 78-81, 94-95 and passim.

12. *Common Ground* 10 (Autumn 1949): 2. As if to show Lincoln's persisting and widespread relevance, the secretary of Chicago's Polonia Society informed President Roosevelt in February 1945 that the society had just celebrated the birthdays of "these great democrats: Lincoln and Kosciuszko." Quoted in Louis L. Gerson, *The Hyphenate in Recent American Politics and Diplomacy* (Lawrence: University of Kansas Press, 1964), p. 173. The naturalization program continued to feature Lincoln's along with other historic figures' statements of American ideals. See Carl B. Hyatt, Director, Attorney General's Citizenship Program, *Gateway to Citizenship* (Washington: Government Printing Office, 1943, 1948), pp. 59, 103, 176.

13. Andrew M. Greeley, *Ethnicity, Denomination, and Inequality* (Beverly Hills: Sage, 1976), pp. 5-12, 45-47, 71.

14. Richard Krickus, *Pursuing the American Dream: White Ethnics and the New Populism* (Bloomington: Indiana University Press, 1976), pp. xii-xiii. Greeley has founded and edits the periodical *Ethnicity,* which, quite unlike *Common Ground,* looks for and stresses signs of persisting ethnic distinctiveness. See also Greeley's *Ethnicity in the United States* (New York: Wiley, 1974).

15. Michael Novak, *The Rise of the Unmeltable Ethnics: Politics and Culture in the Seventies* (New York: Macmillan, 1973), pp. xvii-xviii, 65, 115. Novak himself has "made it" in the academic world, and his own family history involves amalgamation — he has dedicated his book (p. vii) to "the great-grandparents of our children," and these include persons with such names as John Swenson and Dora Carver. To Novak, as to other new ethnic theorists, ethnicity is largely something that one makes up for oneself. He writes, "What is an ethnic group? It is a group with historical memory, real or *imaginary.* One belongs to an ethnic group in part involuntarily, in part *by choice.* Given a grandparent or two, *one chooses* to shape one's consciousness by one history rather than another" (p. 56; italics added). Elsewhere Novak pleads again for a "self-conscious and freely chosen ethnicity" (Novak, "Cultural Pluralism for Individuals: A Social Vision," in Melvin M. Tumin and Walter Plotch, eds., *Pluralism in a Democratic Society* [New York: Praeger, 1977], p. 48).

16. Howard F. Stein and Robert F. Hill, *The Ethnic Imperative: Examining the New White Ethnic Movement* (University Park: Pennsylvania State University Press, 1977), pp. 195-96.

17. For professional educators' endorsements of "cultural pluralism" or "multicultural education," see especially the *Journal of Teacher Edu-*

123

cation (published by the American Association of Colleges for Teacher Education) 24, no. 4 (Winter 1973), and *Educational Leadership: Journal of the Association for Supervision and Curricular Development* 33, no. 3 (December 1975).

18. Lois Buttlar and Lubomyr R. Wynar, *Building Ethnic Collections: An Annotated Guide for School Media Centers and Public Libraries* (Littleton, Colo.: Libraries Unlimited, 1977), pp. 11, 17, and passim.

19. Nathan Glazer, "Cultural Pluralism: The Social Aspect," in Tumin and Plotch, eds., *Pluralism in a Democratic Society*, pp. 17-18. Glazer is professor of psychology at Harvard University. More extensive and highly effective analyses and criticisms of the new trend are to be found in Stein and Hill, *Ethnic Imperative,* and in Orlando Patterson, *Ethnic Chauvinism: The Reactionary Impulse* (New York: Stein and Day, 1977). For dissenting views by educators, see also the educational journals cited in note 17 above; see especially Carl J. Dolce, "Multicultural Education: Some Issues," *Journal of Teacher Education* 24 (Winter 1973): 282-84.

There is no serious objection to ethnic studies as such. Indeed, the role of immigration and of immigrants has been, for much too long, comparatively neglected in the writing and teaching of American history. The doubts and criticisms apply to the particular ways that some advocates would use such studies. These advocates claim to be promoting harmony rather than disunity, but harmony is not likely to arise from teaching each group that it is morally superior to other groups, especially the WASPs (who do not really constitute a single, homogeneous entity at all). The advocates claim to favor the free development of each personality, but individualism will hardly gain from the imposition of ethnic stereotypes. (The kind of Slovakianization that Novak stands for can scarcely be considered an improvement upon the kind of Americanization that the worst of the nativists once advocated.) The democratic ideal is not a society in which each citizen defers to the organizers of some minority group; it is, rather, a society in which each citizen is a minority of one.

20. "No One Model American: A Statement on Multicultural Education," adopted in November 1972 by the AACTE Board of Directors, *Journal of Teacher Education* 24 (Winter 1973): 264-65.

21. Novak, in Tumin and Plotch, eds., *Pluralism in a Democratic Society,* p. 43.

22. Novak, *Rise of the Unmeltable Ethnics,* pp. 202-3. For other flattering references to Kennedy, see pp. 209, 214, 299.

23. Stein and Hill, *Ethnic Imperative,* pp. 106-7. See also pp. 99, 105.

24. Roy P. Basler, Marion Dolores Pratt, and Lloyd A. Dunlap, eds., *The Collected Works of Abraham Lincoln* (New Brunswick, N.J.: Rutgers University Press, 1953-1955), 1:337-38.

25. Lincoln, *Collected Works,* 2:323. For other disavowals of Know-Nothingism, see 2:234, 316, 524, and 3:383. For Lincoln's Chicago speech of July 10, 1858, see 2:499-500.

26. For a collection of the best scholarship on the subject, see Frederick C. Luebke, ed., *Ethnic Voters and the Election of Lincoln* (Lincoln: University of Nebraska Press, 1971), especially pp. xxv-xxxii.

27. Lincoln, *Collected Works,* 4:203.

28. *Seebote,* October 25, 1862, quoted in Mary D. Meyer, "The Germans in Wisconsin and the Civil War: Their Attitude toward the Union, the Republicans, Slavery, and Lincoln" (Master's thesis, Catholic University of America, 1937), pp. 45-46.

29. On immigrant resistance to the draft in Wisconsin, see Richard N. Current, *The History of Wisconsin, Volume II: The Civil War Era, 1848-1873* (Madison: State Historical Society of Wisconsin, 1976), pp. 315-19, 324-27, 331-33. For a brief account of the New York draft riots of 1863, see Fred A. Shannon, *The Organization and Administration of the Union Army, 1861-1865* (Cleveland: Clark, 1928), 2:205-15. For a long and vivid account, see J. T. Headley, *Pen and Pencil Sketches of the Great Riots* (New York: E. B. Treat, 1882; reprint ed., Arno Press/New York Times, 1969), pp. 136-335.

30. Lincoln, *Collected Works,* 6:203-4, 7:38.

31. For a discussion of Lincoln's devotion to the principles of the Declaration and the Constitution, see Richard N. Current, ed., *The Political Thought of Abraham Lincoln* (Indianapolis: Bobbs-Merrill, 1967), pp. xiii-xxxi.

32. J. Hector St. John, *Letters from an American Farmer* (New York: Fox, Duffield, 1904), pp. 54-55. "St. John" was Crèvecoeur's pen name, and the book was originally published in London in 1782. The president of the American Association of Colleges for Teacher Education ignorantly asserts: "The melting pot concept was an historians' invention, a way of looking at society as some men *wished* to see it" (*Journal of Teacher Education* 24 [Winter 1973]: 262). Actually, the concept represents the aspirations of immigrants themselves and has had a long history. In place of the "melting pot," new ethnics would substitute the metaphor of "stew" or a "mosaic."

33. The first of these Lincoln quotations is from his inaugural address, March 4, 1861; the second is from his Springfield address of June 16, 1858. Lincoln, *Collected Works,* 2:461, 4:270.

[IX]

The Lincoln Presidents

EACH OCCUPANT of the White House finds that "all the Presidents who have gone before have left something of themselves behind." There is an "unseen Presidency. Its tradition, experience, judgment, and example speak across the centuries from one President to the next." So one of them has said, at any rate.[1] Certainly they have been fond of quoting or misquoting the statements and recalling with more or less relevance and accuracy the actions of presidents who have gone before.

Abraham Lincoln has remained one of the favorites. In quoting or recalling Lincoln, the twentieth-century presidents have had interests of their own to serve. These men have tried to get his support in their political contests, his justification for their uses of executive power, and his reassurance for their personal qualifications as statesmen. Whatever the immediate concern, when the presidents cite Lincoln they tell us something about the presidency and about political leadership, both in their time and in his.

[1]

The most recent of the Republican presidents, soon after taking office, informed the Congress and the people quite frankly that he

A luncheon talk at the ninth annual National Leadership Symposium, Center for the Study of the Presidency, Springfield, Illinois, November 4, 1978. Reprinted by permission from the *Presidential Studies Quarterly* 9 (Winter 1979): 25-35.

was "a Ford, not a Lincoln."[2] His immediate predecessor, also a member of Lincoln's party, had seen a much closer resemblance between Lincoln and himself. Richard M. Nixon could hear the man who had saved the Union saying to him across the years: "Now save the cause of peace and freedom for the whole world."[3] But the rest of the Republicans, with the exception of Theodore Roosevelt, were rather perfunctory in their references to Lincoln. The Democrats, with the exception of John F. Kennedy, far outdid most of the Republicans in the frequency and fervor with which they invoked the great Republican's name.

Lyndon B. Johnson at first saw himself as a new emancipator. "Abraham Lincoln abolished slavery," Johnson repeatedly declaimed, "and we can abolish poverty." As the war on poverty gave way to the war in Vietnam, the Johnson speechwriters looked for comparisons with Lincoln as a war leader holding together a people weary of sacrifice and impatient for victory. When the escalation was just beginning, Johnson celebrated Lincoln's Birthday with a White House luncheon, to which he invited about a hundred people who had written about Lincoln or had taken his part on stage or screen. He, too, knew something about Lincoln, Johnson told his guests. "And sometimes at night, as I struggle with terrifying problems, his presence in the dark corridors seems to be almost real." Commenting on the occasion, the columnist Mary McGrory wrote that L.B.J. had "stolen Lincoln for his own party and claimed him for his own."[4]

In the midst of the Korean War, when Harry S. Truman was having difficulties with Douglas MacArthur, he remembered Lincoln and *his* troubles with George B. McClellan. And when Truman faced demands for the dismissal of Dean Acheson, he reminded his tormentors of Lincoln's refusal to yield to similar demands in the case of William H. Seward. Truman considered himself a Lincoln Democrat. He said "Lincoln Republicans" were "almost extinct. The rulers of the Republican party long ago repudiated everything Abraham Lincoln stood for, except his sense of humor — and now they are trying to repudiate that."[5]

Whether consciously or not, Truman was echoing Franklin D. Roosevelt. "I think it is time for us Democrats to claim Lincoln as one of our own," Roosevelt had written privately as early as 1929, soon after becoming governor of New York. "The Republican party has certainly repudiated, first and last, everything that he stood for." After becoming president, Roosevelt talked frequently of Lincoln as the first New Dealer. Roosevelt said: "The principle of Andrew Jackson's true democracy came back to life in the White House with the next real Democrat, Abraham Lincoln." Ex-President Herbert Hoover tried to recover Lincoln. "Recently both Mr. Roosevelt and Mr. Browder [Earl Browder, the American Communist party leader] have claimed him as a founder of their faiths," Hoover remarked. "I was under the impression he was a Republican." This rebuke did not deter Roosevelt from going on to identify himself with Lincoln as a wartime commander-in-chief and a savior of democracy.[6]

F.D.R. was not the first Democrat to appropriate Lincoln and identify with him. That honor goes to Woodrow Wilson. "I sometimes think it is a singular circumstance that the present Republican party should have sprung from Lincoln," Wilson said while campaigning for the presidency in 1912, "but that is one of the mysteries of Providence, and for my part I feel the closest kinship in principle and in political lineament to that great mind." Wilson was running as a self-proclaimed outsider (like Jimmy Carter in 1976) and he described Lincoln as an outsider of exactly the same sort. The country needed another Lincoln — that is, a Woodrow Wilson — a man who had "not been associated with the governing classes and influences of this country . . . a voice from the outside."[7] Once elected, Wilson continued to call Lincoln to his aid, first for domestic reforms and then for foreign crusades.

In leading the country to war, however, Wilson was much too hesitant to suit that bellicose Bull Mooser Theodore Roosevelt. Wilson's references to Lincoln and also to George Washington only intensified Roosevelt's fury. "Lip-loyalty to Washington and Lincoln costs nothing and is worth just exactly what it costs," Roosevelt practically screamed. "Whoever is too proud to fight . . . whoever demands peace without victory . . . is false to the teachings and lives of Washington and Lincoln. Whoever seeks office . . . on the ground that he 'kept us out of war' . . . is treacherous to the principles of Washington and Lincoln; *they* did not 'keep us out of war.' "[8]

Earlier Roosevelt had conceded that, before his own presidency, the Republicans themselves had given lip service to Lincoln's name. The party, he explained, had fallen into the hands of conservatives and even reactionaries. "These men still from force of habit applauded what Lincoln had done in the way of radical dealing with the abuses of his day; but they did not apply the spirit in which Lincoln worked to the abuses of their own day."[9]

Historically, it is quite fitting that Democrats in the twentieth century should have claimed the first Republican president, for Republicans in Lincoln's time had asserted exactly the same kind of claim to the first Democratic president. In 1859 Lincoln sent greetings to fellow Republicans who were about to hold a Thomas Jefferson festival in Boston. He said: "It is both curious and interesting that those supposed to descend politically from the party opposed to Jefferson should now be celebrating his birthday . . . while those claiming political descent from him have nearly ceased to breathe his name everywhere." The Jefferson and anti-Jefferson parties had exchanged principles. It reminded Lincoln of "seeing two partially intoxicated men engage in a fight with their greatcoats on, which fight, after a long and rather harmless contest, ended in each having fought himself *out* of his own coat and *into* that of the other."[10]

Lincoln argued that, as advocates of freedom and human rights, he and his partisans were the true inheritors of the Jeffersonian tradition. He averred he was, in some respects, Andrew Jackson's as well as Jefferson's legatee. In reply to Stephen A. Douglas he wrote: "I point out to him that Mr. Jefferson and General Jackson were both against him on the binding political authority of Supreme Court decisions." And Lincoln saw a similarity between himself and Jackson in their common devotion to the Union. But Lincoln did not appeal to the memory of Democratic heroes alone. "*We* stick," he insisted, "to . . . the identical old policy which was adopted by the fathers of the Republic" — by Washington and John Adams as well as Jefferson and James Madison. On February 22 he was moved to exaggeration, just as later politicians were to be on February 12. "To add brightness to the sun, or glory to the name of Washington, is alike impossible."[11]

[2]

When Lincoln referred to the principles and policies of earlier presidents, he was attempting, of course, to enlist the support of their ghosts in the politics of his own time. In the same way his successors tried to get him on their side. They were concerned not only with political issues but also with presidential powers. The men who thought of themselves as "strong" executives, whether Republicans or Democrats, looked for precedents in the Lincoln record.

Writing in 1913, Theodore Roosevelt maintained that the division between strong and weak presidents had normally run along "temperamental" rather than partisan lines. "The course I followed, of regarding the Executive as subject only to the people, and . . . bound to serve the people affirmatively in cases where the Constitution does not explicitly forbid . . . was substantially the course followed by both Andrew Jackson and Abraham Lincoln. Other honorable and well-meaning Presidents, such as James Buchanan, took the . . . narrowly legalistic view that the President is the servant of Congress rather than of the people, and can do nothing . . . unless the Constitution explicitly commands the action." Roosevelt classified his former friend and hand-picked successor William Howard Taft along with Buchanan and called the opposing views of presidential power "the Lincoln-Jackson and the Buchanan-Taft schools." He said the Lincoln-Jackson view would have justified him, if the necessity had arisen, in using the army to take over the coal mines at the time of the anthracite strike of 1902.[12]

Wilson, as a scholar, had pondered the presidents before becoming one of them. Washington, Jackson, and Lincoln he once considered exceptions rather than models. In 1897 he wrote: "Lincoln made the presidency the government while the war lasted . . . but . . . his time was a time of fearful crisis, when men studied power, not law. No one of these men seems the normal President, or affords example of the usual courses of administration." After years of "congressional government," however, Wilson saw a change following the Spanish-American War. "Foreign questions became leading questions," he wrote in 1908, ". . . and in them the President was of necessity leader. Our new place in the affairs of the world has . . . kept him at the front of our government, where our own thoughts and the attention of men everywhere is centred upon him."[13] And before long the attention of men everywhere was centered upon Wilson.

Franklin D. Roosevelt agreed with his cousin Theodore that the real distinction between presidents did not depend on party membership, but F.D.R. categorized them somewhat differently. Writing in 1941, while in his third term, he said that in times of crisis there appeared "usually two general schools of political belief — liberal and conservative. . . . In Jefferson's day, in Jackson's day, and in Lincoln's, and Theodore Roosevelt's, and Wilson's day, one group emerged clearly as liberals." They believed that, "as new conditions and problems arise beyond the power of men and women to meet them as individuals, it becomes the duty of the government" — and, by implication, the duty of the president — "to find new remedies with which to meet them. . . . That theory of the role of government was expressed by Abraham Lincoln when he said, 'The legitimate object of government is to do for a community of people whatever they need to have done but cannot do at all or cannot do so well for themselves in their separate and individual capacities.' "[14]

Truman held an even more expansive notion of executive authority than Theodore Roosevelt had put forth, and though T.R. only threatened to take over the coal mines, Truman actually seized the steel mills to prevent a strike. At a press conference he was asked: "Are there any limitations at all over a President's actions during an emergency?" He replied, in effect, that there were none. "Mr. Lincoln," he explained, "exercised the powers of the President to meet the emergencies with which he was faced."[15]

Truman thought the Korean War justified his seizure of the steel mills. When the steel companies took the case to court, the administration's brief mentioned Lincoln's 1861 seizure of the railroad and telegraph lines between Annapolis and Washington, and it listed his Emancipation Proclamation as another example of divestiture by the executive. "I think the Constitution invests its Commander-in-Chief with the law of war in time of war," the brief went on, quoting Lincoln. "Is there — has there ever been — any question that, by the law of war, property both of enemies and [of] friends may be taken when needed?"[16]

Yet Truman and other assertive presidents, when the mood was on them, pictured Lincoln as something different from an all-powerful commander-in-chief, something less than a man who made the presidency the government. Truman once remarked: "Lincoln had a great deal of trouble with his Cabinet because some of them got it into their heads that they, and not the President, were the policy-makers." Wilson, when trying to discourage Congress from setting up a watchdog committee, warned of the "ominous precedent" of the Committee on the Conduct of War, which he said had "rendered Mr. Lincoln's task all but impossible."[17] That sounds as if Lincoln was really rather frustrated and ineffective as a president.

When it served his interest to do so, even Theodore Roosevelt could drastically revise his view of Lincoln and the presidency. In 1918, attacking Wilson as a would-be wartime dictator, T.R. quoted selectively but at length from the strictures that Congressman Lincoln had laid upon President James K. Polk during the Mexican War. "Remember that this is Lincoln speaking, in wartime, of the President," T.R. said. "The President is merely the most important among a large number of public servants. He should be supported or opposed exactly to the degree which is warranted by his good conduct or bad conduct."[18] Merely one of many public servants? This was not the kind of president that T.R. had described as ideal only five years earlier — the "Lincoln-Jackson" type who could do anything the Constitution did not explicitly forbid and who apparently was his own judge of good and bad conduct.

Ex-President Taft had been amused, in 1913, at T.R.'s designating himself as one of the "Lincoln Presidents" and Taft as one of the "Buchanan Presidents." Turning serious, Taft proceeded to dispute Roosevelt's contention that the executive was supposed "to play the part of a Universal Providence and set all things right." The notion of an "undefined residuum of power" in the executive was an "unsafe doctrine," Taft cautioned. True, under "the stress of the greatest civil war in modern times," Lincoln had taken steps "the constitutionality of which was seriously questioned." But Lincoln "always pointed out the source of the authority which in his opinion justified his acts." He "never claimed that whatever authority in government was not expressly denied to him he could exercise."[19]

In addition to Taft, other Republican presidents believed that Lincoln stood for limited rather than limitless authority. Dwight D. Eisenhower, for one, was even fonder than Franklin D. Roosevelt had been of Lincoln's statement about the "legitimate object of government." But Eisenhower paraphrased the statement in such a way as to give it a quite different meaning from the one that F.D.R. had derived from it. Eisenhower said: "We try to stick to the old Lincolnian dictum that it is the function of government to do for people those things they cannot do for themselves and to stay out of things in places where the people can do things for themselves."[20]

Opponents of the Vietnam war appealed to Lincoln against Johnson and Nixon. If, the objectors reasoned, a president could not seize property — and the Supreme Court had repudiated Truman's seizure of the steel mills — still less could a president seize people for service in an undeclared war. In a suit challenging the constitutionality of the involvement in Vietnam, the American Civil Liberties Union pointed out that Lincoln had challenged the constitutionality of the war with Mexico. The A.C.L.U. brief quoted a letter of Lincoln's denouncing Polk for ordering the invasion of a country with which we were at peace.[21]

So advocates of presidential restraint as well as advocates of presidential assertiveness have made use of Lincoln's name. Which group has the better right to it? Does Lincoln himself qualify as a "Lincoln President," or was he really a "Buchanan President"? Or were there, in reference to this matter of executive authority, two different Lincolns? It almost seems as if there were two of them — the man before 1861, and the man in 1861 and after.

As a Whig, as an opponent of the party of Jackson and Polk, the earlier Lincoln insisted on a strictly limited presidency. He certainly denied that Polk could rightfully make war at will. "Allow the President to invade a neighboring nation whenever *he* shall deem it necessary to repel an invasion, and you allow him to do so *whenever he may choose to say* he deems it necessary for such a purpose — and you allow him to make war at pleasure." Thus Lincoln expostulated to his law partner William Herndon in 1848. The "provision of the Constitution giving the war-making power to Congress," Lincoln went on to explain, was intended to make sure that "*no one man* should hold the power of bringing this oppression on us."[22]

During the presidential campaign of 1848 Lincoln penned some words he hoped the Whig candidate, Zachary Taylor, would utter on the stump: "Finally, were I president, I should desire the legislation of the country to rest with Congress, uninfluenced by the executive in its origin or progress, and undisturbed by the veto unless in very special and clear cases." As late as February 1861, only a few weeks before his inauguration, he reiterated the Whig concept of the president who defers to Congress. "By the constitution, the executive may recommend measures which he may think proper; and he may veto those he thinks improper; and it is supposed he may add to these, certain indirect influences to affect the action of Congress," Lincoln said on the way from Springfield to Washington. "My political education strongly inclines me against a very free use of any of these means, by the Executive, to control the legislation of the country."[23]

Once he was in the White House, Lincoln began to act decisively on his own without first consulting Congress, which for the time being was not in session. Like Polk he sent armed forces into disputed territory, and like Polk he was to be accused of starting a war by maneuvering the other side into firing the first shot. During the opening weeks of the war, when the secessionists seemed on the verge of quickly winning it by taking Maryland and isolating Washington, Lincoln resorted to some drastic measures for saving the Union. Without congressional authorization he enlarged the army and the navy, spent and borrowed money, and suspended the writ of habeas corpus in certain areas, thus making possible the arrest and detention of thousands of people without trial.

To justify his actions, from sending the Fort Sumter expedition to authorizing the arbitrary arrests, Lincoln relied directly or indirectly on the Constitution. That document clearly states that the writ of habeas corpus may be suspended "when in cases of rebellion or invasion the public safety may require it," though the wording leaves in doubt whether the suspension is up to the president or up to the Congress. Besides, the Constitution requires the president to "take care that the laws be faithfully executed," and Lincoln made much of his inaugural oath to "preserve, protect, and defend the Constitution of the United States." To preserve the Constitution as a whole, he was willing temporarily to sacrifice a part of it.[24] When Congress met, he requested and received its authorization for what he had done. Eventually the Supreme Court added its approval.

Lincoln made his most extreme assertion of presidential power when he issued his Emancipation Proclamation. At first he had no inkling that he could issue or authorize such a thing. He disclaimed any authority to do so when, in September 1861, he revoked the emancipation proclamation that General John C. Frémont had issued for the state of Missouri. "Can it be pretended," Lincoln wrote in defense of his revocation, "that it is any longer the government of the U.S. — any government of Constitution and laws — wherein a General, or a President, may make permanent rules of property by proclamation?"[25] By September 1862 he had somehow convinced himself that as commander-in-chief he did, after all, possess a constitutional power, a previously unasserted "war power," which enabled him to proclaim the freedom of all slaves in enemy territory.

Afterward Lincoln sometimes wondered whether he really was entitled to that kind of authority. When he proposed a loyalty oath for ex-rebels, he asked them to swear to abide by his proclamations "having reference to slaves" only "so long and so far as not modified or declared void by decision of the Supreme Court." To the end he remained unsure of the legal scope, duration, and validity of his antislavery edict.[26]

If, indeed, we can properly speak of two Lincolns, the pre-1861 and the post-1861, the two were not nearly so different in principle and practice as they might seem. The man changed much less than the country's situation did. As president, Lincoln not only continued to be aware of constitutional limits on executive action; he also kept up the Whiggish habit of deferring rather than dictating to Congress. He seldom tried to determine legislation, and he almost never used the veto.[27]

[3]

Besides looking to Lincoln for political support and for official precedents, later occupants of the White House have looked to him also for personal reassurance. If he was a great statesman, and if they were statesmen with some title to greatness, they must have shared at least a few of his character traits. Sure enough, each of the supposedly "strong" presidents has found a bit of himself reflected in Lincoln's image. Here are samples of their testimony:

Lincoln was stirred by "a lofty ideal," yet he "accepted human nature" and "worked with keen, practical good sense." He had none of the "diseased morality" that "makes a man in this workday world refuse to do what is possible because he cannot accomplish the impossible."[28] In short, he must have been much like the writer of those words, Theodore Roosevelt.

"It was a very lonely spirit that looked out . . . and comprehended men without fully communing with them, as if, in spite of all its genial efforts at comradeship, it dwelt apart, saw its visions of duty where no man looked on. There is a very holy and very terrible isolation for the conscience of every man who seeks to read the destiny in affairs for others as well as for individuals."[29] In thus describing Lincoln, Woodrow Wilson was also describing himself.

Lincoln "had to compromise to gain a little something. Lincoln was one of those unfortunate people called a 'politician,' but he was a politician who was practical enough to get a great many things done for his country. He was a sad man because he couldn't get it all at once. And nobody can."[30] Not even Franklin D. Roosevelt.

"He had nerve enough to save the Union under the most difficult circumstances. . . . He had the guts to go ahead and do what he thought was the right thing at a time when he had a great big opposition."[31] Lincoln had nerve and guts — just like the feisty Harry S. Truman.

"Lincoln was often racked by doubts. In the conduct of grave human affairs, dogmatic certainty is often the handmaiden of catastrophe. But doubts can lead to disaster too — paralyzing the will when the times cry out for action. The true quality of Lincoln emerges, I think, from the fact that for four long brutal years he never permitted his anguish and doubt to ever deter him from acting."[32] Lincoln had all the doubt and determination of Lyndon B. Johnson.

"He was a very competitive man. . . . He lost elections, and came back to win for the Presidency of the United States. He never gave up."[33] In that description of Lincoln it is easy to recognize Richard M. Nixon.

Of all the men who followed Lincoln to the White House, Wilson had the truest empathy with him (even though Wilson believed "Washington would continue in history the greater man"). Historian and political scientist that he was, Wilson also knew Lincoln best and analyzed his qualities of leadership with the greatest insight. As Wilson saw him, Lincoln mastered people through his mastery of words, his ability to understand and to express the people's "sentiments and aspirations." He led because he could discover and announce "a new principle for a new age"; he could speak what no one else knew — "the common meaning of the common voice." As a manager of men, he had the capacity to "reduce complex situations to their simples." In setting policy, he "was not afraid to take the initiative, but he would not take it rashly or too soon. He governed and succeeded by sympathy."[34]

So Wilson said, and he said much more on the subject, but having done so he confessed his bewilderment. "I have read biographies of Lincoln," he declared; "I have sought out with the greatest interest the many intimate stories that are told of him, the narratives of nearby friends, the sketches at close quarters, in which those who had the privilege of being associated with him have tried to depict for us the very man himself 'in his habit as he lived'; but I have nowhere found a real intimate of Lincoln's. I nowhere get the impression in any narrative or reminiscence that the writer had in fact penetrated to the heart of his mystery, or that any man could penetrate to the heart of it."[35]

As for Lincoln himself, he considered Jefferson the "most distinguished politician of our history." He admired Jackson for the "decision of character that ever characterized him" and that was particularly notable in his handling of the nullification attempt. Lincoln identified with both Washington and Jackson when Maryland secessionists expected him to "surrender the Government

without a blow" soon after the firing on Fort Sumter. He protested: "There is no Washington in that — no Jackson in that —
no manhood nor honor in that."[36] But throughout his career the
politician he felt the closest affinity for was none of the presidential greats. It was, instead, a man who had continually tried to become president and had never succeeded. It was Henry Clay.

Clay was Lincoln's "beau ideal of a statesman" — the one
"whom, during my whole political life, I have loved and revered
as a teacher and leader." In a eulogy soon after Clay's death, in
1852, Lincoln undertook to explain why Clay had been "the most
loved and most implicitly followed by friends, and the most
dreaded by opponents, of all living American politicians." Lincoln
said: "It is probably true he owed his pre-eminence to no one quality, but to a fortunate combination of several. He was surpassingly
eloquent; but many eloquent men fail utterly; and they are not, as
a class, generally successful. His judgment was excellent; but many
men of good judgment live and die unnoticed. His will was in-
domitable; but this quality often secures to its owner nothing better than a character for useless obstinacy." No inventory of Clay's
traits could quite provide the explanation. "The spell — the long
enduring spell — with which the souls of men were bound to him,
is a miracle," Lincoln had to conclude. "Who can compass it?"

Lincoln saw in Clay much of what he was himself and much of
what he aspired to be. Not only was Lincoln's Clay a person of
will, judgment, and eloquence, always speaking in a "deeply earnest and impassioned tone" and in a spirit of "sincerity" and "conviction" that "truly touches the chords of human sympathy." He
was also a man of worthy principles and high ideals, one who devoted himself to the cause of both human liberty and sectional
peace. He "duly weighed every conflicting interest" and was "regarded by all as *the* man for a crisis."[37]

Long before reaching the eminence that Clay never attained,
Lincoln admitted to being a politician and an ambitious one. "Politicians" he once defined as "a set of men who have interests aside
from the interests of the people, and who, to say the most of them,

are, taken as a mass, at least one long step removed from honest men. I say this with the greater freedom because, being a politician myself, none can regard it as personal." But in less cynical moments he insisted that he had public as well as private aims. His greatest ambition, he early announced, was "that of being truly esteemed of my fellow men, by rendering myself worthy of their esteem." Years later, while still acknowledging his "personal ambition," he said he was not in politics "for a mere personal object." He was in it to resist the spread of slavery. He hoped to rise, but he hoped to do it in such a way "that the oppressed of my species might have shared with me in the elevation."[38]

Never did Lincoln show any hankering for the perquisites or trappings of exalted power. If absolute power corrupts absolutely, he was absolutely safe from corruption. As a young man, he warned against future politicians of a dictatorial bent. Men of "ambition and talents" would "seek the gratification of their ruling passion," and in doing it they might someday undermine the American structure of popular government. An ordinary "presidential chair" would hardly satisfy the home-grown equivalent of "an Alexander, a Caesar, or a Napoleon."[39]

[4]

Such, in actual life, were the concerns of the Lincoln whose image, more or less distorted, later presidents were to exploit. When, regardless of their party, they represented themselves as his true followers, they were indeed doing as he had done, for he had said again and again that *he* was the true follower of the honored dead of both parties of the past. But when his successors asserted the broadest presidential power and took him as their prototype, they were making a very dubious use of history and biography. Political scientists as well as politicians have exaggerated his usurpations as president.[40] Neither by word nor by deed did he give any real justification for the idea of "executive privilege" or of an "imperial presidency."

140

Nor, in the example of his personality, does he quite sustain those who consciously or unconsciously have found themselves reflected there. Whatever the secret of his leadership, he seems to have had in full measure at least one quality that all the others lacked in some degree. This was not humility or even modesty but a kind of ego perspective, an ability to see himself accurately in relation to people around him. It kept him well away from delusions of grandeur. So did his conception of what a statesman ought to be like. Who else among the presidents has idolized a politician who failed even to make it to the White House?

NOTES

1. Remarks broadcast on a program sponsored by the Democratic Victory Committee, November 3, 1968, in *Public Papers of the Presidents of the United States: Lyndon B. Johnson* (Washington: Government Printing Office, 1965-70), 10:1110-11. "To Charles Maguire fell the task of writing the speech and coordinating its production." George Christian, *The President Steps Down: A Personal Memoir of the Transfer of Power* (New York: Macmillan, 1970), pp. 169-70.

2. Address to a joint session of Congress, August 12, 1974, in *Public Papers of the Presidents of the United States: Gerald R. Ford* (Washington: Government Printing Office, 1975-77), 1:7.

3. Remarks at a ceremony commemorating Lincoln's birth, February 12, 1974, in *Public Papers of the Presidents of the United States: Richard M. Nixon* (Washington: Government Printing Office, 1971-75), 6:156-58.

4. See Johnson's remarks in Albuquerque, New Mexico, October 24, 1964; at the White House luncheon, February 12, 1965; and at Lincoln's Birthday celebration, February 12, 1968, in *Public Papers ... Johnson*, 2:1488, 3:180-81, 9:218-19. On the luncheon, see also Eric F. Goldman, *The Tragedy of Lyndon Johnson* (New York: Knopf, 1969), pp. 277-78, and Lady Bird Johnson, *A White House Diary* (New York: Holt, 1970), pp. 242-43. Goldman quotes McGrory. He says he himself wrote a speech for the occasion, but "the President scrapped my version almost completely" and went ahead on his own. Christian, *President Steps Down*, refers to the tactics of Johnson's advisors and speechwriters from 1966 on: "Walt Rostow and others dug up historical records of similar impatience in previous wars, especially in the terrible times Lincoln had in holding the North together when a speedy victory did not come about" (p. 120).

5. The quotation is from a campaign speech for Adlai Stevenson in Spokane, Washington, October 1, 1952, in *Public Papers of the Presidents of the United States: Harry S. Truman* (Washington: Government Printing Office, 1961-66), 8:670. On McClellan-MacArthur and Seward-Acheson, see Truman's response at a news conference, December 19, 1950, in *Public Papers . . . Truman,* 6:751. See also Truman, *Memoirs* (New York: Doubleday, 1955-56), 1:119-21, 2:429, 442-43; and Merle Miller, *Plain Speaking: An Oral Biography of Harry S. Truman* (New York: Berkley, 1973), pp. 344-47.

6. Roosevelt to Claude G. Bowers, April 3, 1929, in Donald Day, *Franklin D. Roosevelt's Own Story* (Boston: Little, Brown, 1951), p. 120; Roosevelt's Jackson Day dinner address, Washington, D.C., January 7, 1939, in *The Public Papers and Addresses of Franklin D. Roosevelt* (New York: Random, Macmillan, Harper, 1938-50), 8:65; Hoover's address to the National Republican Club, New York City, at a Lincoln Day dinner, February 13, 1939, in Hoover, *Further Addresses upon the American Road, 1939-1940* (New York: Scribner's, 1940), p. 58; Alfred H. Jones, *Roosevelt's Image Brokers: Poets, Playwrights, and the Use of the Lincoln Symbol* (Port Washington, N.Y.: Kennikat, 1974), pp. 3-4, 64-69, 113. Jones is especially concerned with the influence of Carl Sandburg, Stephen Vincent Benét, and Robert E. Sherwood on both Lincoln's reputation and Roosevelt's.

7. Lincoln's Birthday address, Chicago, February 12, 1912, in Wilson, *College and State: Educational, Literary and Political Papers (1875-1913),* ed. Ray Stannard Baker and William E. Dodd (New York: Harper, 1925), 2:389; address at Springfield, Illinois, October 9, 1912, in *A Crossroads of Freedom, The 1912 Campaign Speeches of Woodrow Wilson,* ed. John W. Davidson (New Haven: Yale University Press, 1956), pp. 395-96.

8. Theodore Roosevelt, "Washington and Lincoln: The Great Examples," in his *The Foes of Our Household* (New York: Doran, 1917), ch. 4, reprinted in *The Works of Theodore Roosevelt* (New York: Scribner's, 1923-26), 21:56.

9. Theodore Roosevelt, "The Presidency: Making an Old Party Progressive," *Outlook* 105 (November 22, 1913): 634.

10. Lincoln to Henry L. Pierce et al., April 6, 1859, in Roy P. Basler, Marion Dolores Pratt, and Lloyd A. Dunlap, eds., *The Collected Works of Abraham Lincoln* (New Brunswick, N.J.: Rutgers, 1953-55), 3:374-76.

11. Address to the Washington Temperance Society, Springfield, Illinois, February 22, 1842; speech at Olney, Illinois, September 20, 1856; speech at Chicago, July 10, 1858; notes for speeches [ca. August 21, 1858]; speech at Beloit, Wisconsin, October 1, 1859; article written or authorized by Lincoln in the *Illinois State Journal* (Springfield), September 6, 1860, in Lincoln, *Collected Works,* 1:279; 2:378, 496, 552; 3:484; 4:111-12.

12. Roosevelt, "The Presidency," pp. 637-38, 640, 642.

13. Wilson, "Mr. Cleveland as President," *Atlantic Monthly* (March 1897), reprinted in *College and State* 1:286-87; Wilson, *Constitutional Government in the United States* (New York: Columbia University Press, 1917), pp. 57-59.

14. Roosevelt's introduction to the volume, dated June 16, 1941, *Public Papers . . . of Franklin D. Roosevelt*, 7:xxviii-xxx. Roosevelt used the "legitimate object of government" quotation on a number of other occasions, e.g., in a "fireside chat," September 30, 1934, and in an address at Marietta, Ohio, July 8, 1938 (ibid., 3:422, 7:429).

15. News conference, April 24, 1952, in *Public Papers . . . Truman*, 8:295-96. See also his remarks at a news conference on May 22, 1952, ibid., 8:362.

16. Maeva Marcus, *Truman and the Steel Seizure Case: The Limits of Presidential Power* (New York: Columbia University Press, 1977), pp. ix-xi, 155, 322-23.

17. Truman, *Memoirs*, 1:328; Wilson to Representative A. F. Lever, published in *New York Times*, July 24, 1917, and reprinted in Ray Stannard Baker, *Woodrow Wilson, Life and Letters: War Leader, April 6, 1917 — February 28, 1918* (New York: Doubleday, 1939), p. 185. Wilson was objecting to a food-control bill provision for a joint committee on expenditures in the conduct of the war.

18. "Lincoln and Free Speech," *Kansas City Star*, April 6, May 7, 1918, reprinted in *Works of Theodore Roosevelt*, 21:327-28.

19. Taft, *Our Chief Magistrate and His Powers* (New York: Columbia University Press, 1916), pp. 143-48. Earlier, when T.R. was still president and Taft still his loyal aide, Taft had said: "Roosevelt leads his party as Lincoln led his" (speech before the Young Men's Republican Club of Missouri, Kansas City, February 10, 1908, in Taft, *Present-Day Problems: A Collection of Addresses Delivered on Various Occasions* [New York: Dodd, Mead, 1908], p. 289).

20. Remarks at the Conference for the Advertising Council, Washington, D.C., April 3, 1956, in *Public Papers of the Presidents of the United States: Dwight D. Eisenhower* (Washington: Government Printing Office, 1960-61), 4:360. For some other occasions on which Eisenhower quoted or paraphrased the same Lincoln statement, see ibid., 2:245, 286, 771, 856; 3:181, 213, 267; 4:224, 885; 5:99-100, 235; 7:20; 8:138, 335, 377. See also Eisenhower, *The White House Years: Mandate for Change, 1953-1956* (Garden City, N.Y.: Doubleday, 1963), p. 376.

21. Leon Friedman and Burt Newborne, *Unquestioning Obedience to the President: The ACLU Case against the Illegal War in Vietnam* (New York: Norton, 1972), pp. 25, 29, 135-36, 172-73.

22. Lincoln to Herndon, February 15, 1848, in Lincoln, *Collected Works*, 1:451-52.

23. "What General Taylor Ought to Say," [March?] 1848; campaign speech for Taylor at Worcester, Massachusetts, September 12, 1848;

speech at Pittsburgh, February 15, 1861, in Lincoln, *Collected Works,* 1:454, 2:2, 4:214-15. Once Taylor was president, Lincoln thought he ought to assume a little more Jacksonian and a little less Whiggish bearing. "He must occasionally say, 'By the Eternal,' 'I take the responsibility,' " Lincoln wrote to J. M. Clayton, July 28, 1849, "Those phrases were the 'Samson's locks' of Gen. Jackson, and we dare not disregard the lessons of experience" (Lincoln, *Collected Works,* 2:60).

24. Message to Congress in special session, July 4, 1861, in Lincoln, *Collected Works,* 4:428-31.

25. Lincoln to O. H. Browning, September 22, 1861, ibid., 4:532.

26. Lincoln's proclamation of amnesty and reconstruction, December 8, 1863, ibid., 7:54. According to Alexander H. Stephens's account of Lincoln's conversation at the Hampton Roads conference, February 3, 1865, Lincoln confessed he was not sure of the extent of the permanent effect of the Emancipation Proclamation. "Mr. Lincoln said, that was a judicial question. How the Courts would decide it, he did not know, and could give no answer" (Stephens, *A Constitutional View of the Late War Between the States* [Philadelphia: National, 1868-70], 2:610-11).

27. David Donald has described Lincoln as essentially a Whig type of president, and Clinton Rossiter has seen him as a Jacksonian type. His presidency was a "paradox," Donald says. He "drastically extended the range of executive power." "Less than any other major American President," however, "did Lincoln control or even influence the Congress." Rossiter says: "The reaction to Jackson's Presidency was pronounced and prolonged; it was still in progress when Lincoln entered the White House." Yet the "Jacksonian theory of the office prevailed, and Lincoln . . . drew upon it resolutely in his hour of need." See Donald, "Abraham Lincoln: Whig in the White House," in *The Enduring Lincoln,* ed. Norman A. Graebner (Urbana: University of Illinois Press, 1959), pp. 62-63, and Rossiter, *The American Presidency* (New York: Harcourt, 1960), p. 98.

28. Preface to an edition of Lincoln's writings, published in 1905, in *Works of Theodore Roosevelt,* 12:446-47.

29. Acceptance of the Lincoln Memorial, Hodgenville, Kentucky, September 4, 1916, in Wilson, *The New Democracy: Presidential Messages, Addresses, and Other Papers,* ed. Ray Stannard Baker and William E. Dodd (New York: Harper, 1926), 2:295.

30. Press conference, June 5, 1940, in Thomas H. Greer, *What Roosevelt Thought: The Social and Political Ideas of Franklin D. Roosevelt* (East Lansing: Michigan State University Press, 1958), pp. 130-31.

31. Miller, *Plain Speaking,* pp. 436-37.

32. Remarks at a ceremony at the Lincoln Memorial, Washington, D.C., February 12, 1967, in *Public Papers . . . Johnson,* 7:177.

33. Remarks on signing the bill establishing the Lincoln Home National Historic Site in Springfield, Illinois, August 16, 1971, in *Public Pa-*

pers . . . Nixon, 3:899. Nixon is also quoted interestingly on Lincoln and leadership in Earl Mazo, *Richard Nixon: A Political and Personal Portrait* (New York: Harper, 1959), pp. 285-86.

34. Wilson, *Division and Reunion, 1829-1889* (New York: Longmans, Green, 1893), pp. 216-18; "The Reconstruction of the Southern States," *Atlantic Monthly,* January 1901, reprinted in *College and State,* 1:371-72; conversation with E. M. House, September 9, 1917, on Lincoln and Washington, as reported in *The Intimate Papers of Colonel House,* ed. Charles Seymour (Boston: Houghton Mifflin, 1926-28), 3:176-77. The conversation continued: "I repeated . . . that a Massachusetts historian had made the statement that Lincoln would never have been great by his deeds, but it was what he had written that had impressed the world. . . . The President did not agree with this. He thought Lincoln's deeds entitled him to greatness as well as what he wrote. He thought that his environment was, to a certain extent, limited and that by lack of wider education he did not have the outlook he might otherwise have had. Yet he thought his judgment would have been equal to any situation that might have confronted him."

35. Acceptance of the Lincoln Memorial, Hodgenville, Kentucky, September 4, 1916, in Wilson, *New Democracy,* 2:295.

36. Speech at Peoria, October 16, 1854; speech at Princeton, Illinois, July 4, 1856; reply to Baltimore committee, April 22, 1861, in Lincoln, *Collected Works,* 2:249, 346; 4:341.

37. Eulogy on Henry Clay, July 6, 1852; Lincoln to Daniel Ullmann, February 1, 1861, in Lincoln, *Collected Works,* 2:122, 125-26; 4:184.

38. To the People of Sangamon County, March 9, 1832; speech in the Illinois Legislature on the State Bank, January 11, 1837; fragment on Stephen A. Douglas [December 1856?]; notes for speeches [ca. August 21, 1858], in Lincoln, *Collected Works,* 1:8, 65-66; 2:382-83, 548.

39. "The Perpetuation of Our Political Institutions," address before the Young Men's Lyceum of Springfield, Illinois, January 27, 1838, in Lincoln, *Collected Works,* 1:113-14.

40. For a judicious appraisal of Lincoln's use of power, see J. G. Randall, *Constitutional Problems under Lincoln* (Urbana: University of Illinois Press, 1951), pp. 513-22. See also Arthur M. Schlesinger, Jr., *The Imperial Presidency* (Boston: Houghton Mifflin, 1973), pp. 64-67. In the Prize Cases (1863) the Supreme Court upheld Lincoln's use of power. "Since the majority in the Prize Cases confined its endorsement of the war power to the circumstances of ongoing domestic insurrection (or invasion)," Schlesinger points out, "it is hard to see, as later commentators have claimed, that the decision conferred special authority on Presidents in peacetime or in relation to foreign wars."

〚 X 〛

Lincoln the Southerner

"HE WAS REFERRED to as a Southerner by some and even by himself." So declared the foremost Abraham Lincoln authority, James G. Randall, a generation ago. "Lincoln was born in the South," Randall elaborated. That is, of course, he was born in Kentucky ("which, as no one will deny, is a Southern state") to parents who had come from Virginia. True, the family left Kentucky when Abraham was only seven, but as a youth in Indiana and even as a grown man in Illinois he was "still immersed in Southern influences." His Indiana and Illinois homes lay within a "broadly Southern region," one "whose people and habits were Southern," or "predominantly so," and his Kentucky ties remained strong, gaining reinforcement as they did from his marriage connection with the Lexington Todds, "a prominent family of the old South."

Southerner that he was by birth and background, Lincoln, according to Randall, continued throughout his life to think and talk like one. He "used the Southern vernacular." "One could even speak of Lincoln's political views as Southern." As an Illinois politician, "at least down to the late forties," he was a "Clay Whig, which meant that he was at one with the large and influential

Thirteenth annual Rembert W. Patrick Lecture, Guilford College, Greensboro, North Carolina, March 3, 1982. Here published for the first time.

146

brotherhood of Southern Whigs." He was never an abolitionist. "Abolitionist radicals of the prewar, wartime, and postwar era were the precise opposites of Lincoln." As president, he planned an "easy reconstruction," a generous peace, for the South. But he was "confronted with the hateful opposition of anti-Southern radicals" who frustrated his purpose.[1]

[1]

The conception of Lincoln as a man of Southern character and pro-Southern leanings had developed long before Randall gave the idea a well-rounded expression in 1945. In the days immediately following the assassination a number of newspapers, both Northern and Southern, editorialized on the theme that, in losing Lincoln, the South had lost a friend. The *New York Evening Post,* for one, observed: "The whole nation mourns the death of the President, but no part of it ought to mourn that death more keenly than our brothers of the South, who had more to expect from his clemency and sense of justice than from any other man who could succeed to his position." In time the leaders of the late Confederacy, Alexander H. Stephens and then Jefferson Davis, took up the theme. By 1909, the centenary of Lincoln's birth, the feeling of "kinship with Lincoln" had become widespread among Southerners, according to the University of North Carolina historian J. G. deRoulhac Hamilton. He explained that many Southerners had come to admire Lincoln and to identify with him because, for one thing, they realized that he had shared their "belief in the natural inferiority of the negro" and that, if he had lived, he would have been able to "check the radicals in Congress" so as to save the reconstructed states from the horrors of Negro rule.[2]

In the early 1900's Thomas Dixon, Jr., a native Tar Heel, filled out the picture of Lincoln the Southerner in a succession of novels which formed the basis for D. W. Griffith's epoch-making 1915 movie *The Birth of a Nation,* idealizing the Ku Klux Klan. In Dixon's story of *The Clansman* (1905) a South Carolina lady appeals to Lincoln and readily obtains a pardon for her soldier son as the war ends. After God-blessing Lincoln she says: "I must tell you, Mr. President, how surprised and how pleased I am to find you are a Southern man." He asks: "Why, didn't you know that my parents were Virginians, and that I was born in Kentucky?" The lady: "Very few people in the South know it. I am ashamed to say I did not." Lincoln: "Then, how did you know I am a Southerner?" The lady: "By your looks, your manner of speech, your easy, kindly ways."[3]

Competing with the concept of Lincoln the Southerner was the concept of Lincoln the Westerner. This idea, which developed in the North, received the early support of famous poets. In a funeral oration Ralph Waldo Emerson recalled the disappointment of Easterners at the 1860 nomination of Lincoln, the Western candidate. James Russell Lowell wrote of Nature's having molded him from the "sweet clay" of the "unexhausted West." Walt Whitman once referred to him as "the mighty Westerner." On other occasions, however, Whitman took a different view. In a lecture first delivered in 1879 he asked his audience: "Have you never realized it, my friends, that Lincoln, though grafted on the West, is essentially, in personnel and character, a Southern contribution?" A few years later the veteran journalist George Alfred Townsend ("Gath"), a former Lincoln acquaintance, cautioned: "Western and Northern-bred men ought not to forget that Lincoln was of the South." Soon, however, the University of Wisconsin historian Frederick Jackson Turner reemphasized the Western aspect. "In the Civil War the Northwest furnished the national hero," Turner said in 1896, "— Lincoln was the very flower of frontier training and ideals."[4] As Turner's frontier interpretation of American history spread, so did his conception of Lincoln the classic frontiersman.

Still, the image of Lincoln that came to prevail in the early twentieth century was not so much that of the Westerner or the Southerner as the American. "He is the true history of the American people in his time," Emerson had declared in 1865. "New birth of our new soil, the first American," Lowell called him. Lowell found the source of Lincoln's Americanness in his Western background, and so did Turner, who saw him as embodying the nationalism of the Ohio Valley frontier. His Southern admirers, too, hailed him as the preeminent American type, but they ignored the Western elements and made a great deal of his Southern inheritance. He was "the first typical American," the Georgian Henry W. Grady proclaimed in "The New South" address at the New England Club of New York in 1886. He was "the sum of Puritan and Cavalier," Grady said, yet he was "greater than Puritan, greater than Cavalier, in that he was American." Lowell and Grady were correct in calling him "the first American," wrote the North Carolinian Hamilton in his 1909 appreciation of Lincoln. Southerners by then felt a kinship with him not only because they shared his low opinion of the Negro but also because they shared his strong sense of nationalism — "the South of to-day is national."[5]

The most eloquent words on Lincoln as a symbol of American nationality came not from a Southerner or a Northerner but from an Englishman, Lord Charnwood, whose Lincoln biography appeared in 1917. "Americans are fond of discussing Americanism," Charnwood observed. "Very often they select as a pattern of it Abraham Lincoln, the man who kept the North together but has been pronounced to have been a Southerner in his inherited character." Charnwood ended his book with a moving peroration:

> This most unrelenting enemy to the project of the Confederacy was the one man who had quite purged his heart and mind from hatred or even anger towards his fellow-countrymen of the South. That fact came to be seen in the South too, and generations in America are likely to remember it when all other features of his statecraft have grown indistinct. A thousand reminiscences ludicrous or pathetic, passing into myth but enshrining hard fact, will prove to them that this great feature of his policy was a matter of more than policy. They will remember it as adding a peculiar lustre to the renovation of their national existence; as no small part of the glory, surpassing that of former wars, which has become the common heritage of North and South.[6]

Lincoln did not stand alone, however, as a symbol of sectionalism forgotten and nationalism renewed. By the early 1900's the Confederate hero Robert E. Lee had been transformed into a national hero. He was now de-Southernized, in much the same way that Lincoln had already been de-Northernized. He was *Lee the American,* in the title of the New Englander Gamaliel Bradford's admiring biography (1912). The *Chautauquan* of New York welcomed him as a member of "the first triumvirate of greatness," along with Lincoln and George Washington.[7] And all three had in common a Virginia patrimony.

Eventually, by the 1930's, there were more Northerners who revered the memory of Lee than Southerners who revered the memory of Lincoln, and as a rule these Southerners placed him distinctly second to Lee. They were inclined to be of two minds about Lincoln, for while remembering the might-have-been of a generous peace, they could not entirely forget the fact of the war and his responsibility, as they believed, for starting it. Some still repeated the old rumor that he was really Jefferson Davis's half-brother, the illegitimate as contrasted with the legitimate Southern president. Lincoln, then, remained a sectional as well as a national hero, one less honored in the South than in the rest of the country. Of all the former Confederate states, only Tennessee displayed memorials to him, and only Tennessee observed his birthday as an official holiday.[8]

Thus Lincoln had already acquired a reputation as a Southerner — though, in the South, a reputation inferior to that of Davis or Lee — by the time James G. Randall delivered his 1945 lectures on "Lincoln and the South." Addressing a Southern audience at Louisiana State University, Randall made a much more thorough and scholarly elaboration of the theme than anyone had ever done. Indeed, he presented the strongest possible case for Lincoln as a man of Southern antecedents, traits, principles, and sympathies.

During the next three decades no one challenged Randall's overall view of Lincoln as a Southerner. A number of historians, however, undertook to refute the thesis — which had so endeared

Lincoln to generations of white Southerners — that he was pro-Southern (or anti-black) in his Reconstruction aims. Randall's own brilliant disciple David Donald began the revision with an essay on "The Radicals and Lincoln" in 1956. Donald argued that Randall and others had overstated the antagonism between Lincoln and the Radicals and that, in fact, Lincoln and the Radical leader Charles Sumner, at the time of Lincoln's death, had been "working toward an agreement" on black rights in the South.[9] Before long, some historians were describing Lincoln himself as virtually a Radical on the race question.

The idea of Lincoln the Reconstruction Radical also had a long history. In September 1865, about five months after Lincoln's death, the *New York Tribune* published a letter that he ostensibly had written to General James S. Wadsworth before Wadsworth's death in early 1864. According to the *Tribune*'s quotation of him, Lincoln had written of "exacting" suffrage for the freed slaves and serving as "the nation's guardian of these people." An article in *Scribner's Magazine* in 1893 quoted Lincoln, further, as telling General Wadsworth that the "restoration of the Rebel States to the Union must rest upon the principle of civil and political equality of both races."[10]

Not until the 1960's and 1970's did many writers take up the notion of Lincoln the determined advocate of equal rights. Then, for a while, some of them used the Wadsworth letter to clinch the argument. But in 1966 a professor at the College of William and Mary, Ludwell H. Johnson, questioned the authenticity of key parts of the document. Most writers on the subject thought they found plenty of other evidence for Lincoln's radicalism, and they continued to describe him as the friend of aspiring blacks, rather than the friend of reactionary whites, in the postwar South. One, dismissing the Wadsworth letter as irrelevant, stoutly maintained the already current "proposition that Lincoln was moving toward equal rights for Negroes in the southern states as a condition for reconstruction."[11] Another, in a book entitled *The Radical Republicans: Lincoln's Vanguard for Racial Justice* (1969), said Lincoln was al-

151

ways "not far behind his radical critics" and "shortly before his death he prepared to catch up with the radicals once again."[12] Thus, a century after Lincoln's death, there was beginning to prevail an interpretation of his Reconstruction policy quite different from the one that had been intellectually fashionable at the centenary of his birth.

[2]

What of Lincoln's public image and his self-image in his own life-time? Did he see himself, and did his contemporaries see him, as a Southerner by virtue of his Virginia ancestry, his Kentucky birth, and his Indiana upbringing? Did he follow Southern principles in prewar politics and feel Rebel sympathies while a wartime president? Did others perceive him as doing so? These questions need to be answered in the light of authentic records.

As a young man, Lincoln learned that his father's ancestry led back to Pennsylvania and, beyond that, possibly to New England. While he was in Congress, in 1848, he received an inquiry about his genealogy from one of the Massachusetts Lincolns, to whom he was in fact distantly related. "We have a vague tradition, that my great-grand father went from Pennsylvania to Virginia; and that he was a quaker," Lincoln responded. "Further back than this, I have never heard any thing." He showed considerable interest in his Lincoln ancestors, and eventually he realized that his grand-father as well as his great-grandfather had been Pennsylvanian by birth, though he never succeeded in making the Massachusetts connection.[13]

When, as a rising presidential contender in 1859, he prepared an autobiographical sketch for his friend and promoter Jesse W. Fell, he mentioned the Pennsylvania background of his forebears and added: "An effort to identify them with the New-England family of the same name ended in nothing more definite than a similarity of Christian names in both families, such as Enoch, Levi, Mordecai, Solomon, Abraham, and the like." Fell had requested

152

the autobiography for political use, especially in Pennsylvania, and he published it in the *Chester County Times* of that state. Early in 1860, urging Lincoln's "availability" for the Republican nomination, the *Chicago Tribune* suggested that his antecedents were "such as to commend him heartily to the support of Pennsylvania and New Jersey." Later that year a campaign biography hinted at the same thing when it pointed out: "Mr. Lincoln's earlier ancestors were members of the Society of Friends, and went to Virginia from Berks County, Pennsylvania, where some of the family still reside."[14]

Various New Englanders, when they first met Lincoln, commented on what struck them as his Yankee qualities. The newly elected Massachusetts Governor John A. Andrew told him in 1860: "We claim you, Mr. Lincoln, as coming from Massachusetts, because all [those of] the old Lincoln name are from Plymouth Colony." To that, Lincoln politely said: "We'll consider it so this evening." An Englishman, after interviewing him later in the White House, concluded that his physical and mental characteristics, though modified by the American environment, were essentially those of "the yeomen of the north of England — the district from which Lincoln's name suggests that his forefathers came."[15]

It was good politics, of course, to present the Republican candidate in 1860 as a man of Pennsylvania blood and Massachusetts character. Still, it was not entirely a misrepresentation of his personal feelings. In his nonpolitical correspondence he seemed more interested in his Pennsylvania than in his Virginia ancestry.[16] Certainly he was quite aware that he had a Northern lineage.

Lincoln's more immediate Kentucky background did give him, on a few occasions, a pro-Southern reputation. It briefly caused suspicion even among his fellow Illinois Whigs. "I must confess I am afraid of 'Abe,' " the Galena newspaperman Charles Ray confided to Illinois Congressman Elihu B. Washburne in 1854, several months after the Kansas-Nebraska Act had reopened the territorial controversy and alarmed the advocates of Free Soil. "He is Southern by birth, Southern in his associations and Southern, if I mistake not, in his sympathies," Ray explained. "I have thought that he would not come squarely up to the mark in a hand to hand fight with Southern influence and dictation. His wife, you know, is a Todd, of a proslavery family, and so are all his kin."[17] Ray was a fairly recent arrival in Illinois, having come from New York. Though he had met Lincoln, he was not well acquainted with him. Ray was soon to change his mind about him.

Lincoln's Kentucky background later served as a political argument for him rather than against him. After his election to the presidency, when Southerners were denouncing him as no better than an abolitionist, Cassius M. Clay of Kentucky undertook to reassure them in a public letter. "Lincoln is a Kentuckian by birth," Clay reminded them, "and has a Kentucky-born wife, and numerous slaveholding relatives." He "is an old Henry Clay Whig — a conservative by temperament, antecedents, and avowals." He may be counted upon to protect "all the constitutional rights of the South."[18] Lincoln himself made no public statement at the time.

An old Henry Clay Whig he had indeed been, one who yielded to no other in devotion to Clay and Clay's principles. These called for government aid to business through protective tariffs, internal improvements, and a national bank. Campaigning for Clay for president in 1844, Lincoln elaborated on the program in a speech-making tour that took him throughout Illinois and into Indiana. In his speeches he "evinced a thorough mastery of the principles of political economy," as his 1860 biography was to say. But he did not think of the principles as Southern, nor did he think of the Whig candidate as such. "Henry Clay belongs to the country — to the world," Lincoln declared in a eulogy after Clay's death in 1852. "His career has been national."[19]

Neither Lincoln's Kentucky background nor his Kentucky associations kept him from deploring the peculiar institution of the South. His growing dislike of slavery put a strain on his long, close friendship with the Kentuckian Joshua F. Speed, his one-time Springfield roommate. "I do oppose the extension of slavery, because my judgment and feelings so prompt me," Lincoln wrote to

Speed in 1855. "If for this you and I must differ, differ we must."[20] He was being estranged from his Kentucky friend and from Kentucky itself.

Lincoln developed an ambivalence toward his native state. He showed this when, in 1859, he directed some remarks from Cincinnati to the other side of the Ohio River. "I say . . . to the Kentuckians, that I am what they call . . . a 'Black Republican.' I think Slavery is wrong, morally and politically. . . . I say to you, Kentuckians, that I understand you differ radically with me upon this proposition." Thus, for the moment, the people of his native state were to Lincoln "they" and "you," not "we" or "us." Then, before ending the speech, he referred to them as "my brother Kentuckians."[21] He seemed unsure of his own identity.

In his attitude toward Kentucky he continued to waver. "You suggest that a visit to the place of my nativity might be pleasant to me," he replied, after his presidential nomination, to a Kentucky correspondent. "Indeed it would. But would it be safe? Would not the people Lynch me?" On several occasions afterward he "*playfully*" told of the invitation and his response, and soon the *New York Herald* reported that Lincoln thought the invitation a kind of death trap. Much embarrassed, he took pains to get the story corrected.[22]

And when he spoke in Cincinnati again, on the way to his inauguration, he once more addressed the people across the river, this time as "Fellow citizens of Kentucky — friends — brethren." He assured them that the Republicans would not interfere with slavery in Kentucky or in any other state. With him he had the draft of another speech, one he would have delivered inside Kentucky (on his fifty-second birthday) if he had had a chance to do so. In this speech he defended his right, as the duly elected president, to take office without making concessions and yielding to threats. "What Kentuckian, worthy of his birth place, would not do this?" he pleaded. "Gentlemen, I too, am a Kentuckian."[23]

Even if Lincoln had fully and consistently identified with Kentuckians, he would not necessarily have been identifying with

155

Southerners. To him, Kentucky was not, strictly speaking, one of the Southern states. It was one of "the border States, so called — in fact, the middle states," as he indicated in his July 4, 1861, message to Congess.[24]

Lincoln retained much more fond and vivid memories of Indiana than of Kentucky. In Kentucky, after all, he had spent only a few years of early childhood; in Indiana he had lived from the age of seven to the age of twenty-one. He recalled that the Lincoln family had moved away from Kentucky because of dissatisfaction there, "partly on account of slavery; but chiefly on account of the difficulty of land titles." He never saw the South beyond Kentucky until, when nineteen, he made a flatboat trip downriver to New Orleans. Whatever his impressions were on that occasion, they were the impressions of a Hoosier farm youth. When campaigning for Clay in 1844, he revisited the Indiana scenes of his boyhood, and they inspired him to several stanzas of sentimental verse.[25] Kentucky never had any such effect on him.

Toward Hoosiers Lincoln displayed no such ambivalence as toward Kentuckians. His Indiana identification was clear and uncomplicated. Speaking in Indianapolis in 1859, he said "he grew up to his present enormous height on our own good soil of Indiana," and his audience laughed good naturedly. Responding to an invitation from Spencer County, Indiana, in 1860, he wrote: "I would much like to visit the old home, and old friends of my boyhood, but I fear the chance for doing so soon, is not very good."[26] He made no jokes about the danger of being lynched in Indiana.

In his 1860 autobiography Lincoln gave considerably more attention to his Indiana years than to his Kentucky years, and much more to his Illinois years than to the others combined. Home to him was Springfield. "Here I have lived a quarter of a century, and have passed from a young to an old man," he told his fellow Springfielders as he took the train for Washington in 1861. "Here my children have been born, and one is buried."[27] Understandably, he had a much stronger attachment to Illinois than to any other state.

While thinking of himself as, most intimately, an Illinoisan, Lincoln thought of himself as, more broadly, a Westerner. He made a point of his Western background in one of his 1858 debates with Stephen A. Douglas. Speaking in Jonesboro, near the southern tip of Illinois, Lincoln implied a personal contrast with Douglas's Eastern background. "Mr. Lincoln attempts to cover up and get over his abolitionism by telling you that he was raised a little to the east of you, beyond the Wabash in Indiana," Douglas retorted. "I do not know that the place where a man is born or raised has much to do with his political principles. . . . True, I was not born out west here. I was . . . born in a valley in Vermont."[28]

Backers of Lincoln for president made much of his Western identity. One of his earliest and most earnest promoters, taking up his cause in 1859, was the same Charles Ray who five years before had objected to him as too much a Southern man. Now, as co-owner and co-editor of the powerful *Chicago Tribune,* Ray was supporting him with the argument that he was not only a sound Republican but also a Western man. "It is not enough that the West should be allowed to furnish a Western candidate with *Southern principles,*" Ray editorialized, and his readers could quickly catch the reference to Douglas. "Let us have a Western statesman who will remember there is a West, whose interests are entitled to full and equal care and attention at the hands of the Executive and Congress."[29] Readers did not have to guess that the statesman Ray had in mind was Lincoln.

An 1860 campaign biography, while making a brief reference to Lincoln's Pennsylvania descent, expatiated on his Western nature, with quotations from men who knew (or at least had met) him. According to these authorities, he talked like a Westerner — "his conversation savors strongly of Western idioms and pronunciation." His "great heart and vigorous intellect" had been "allowed a generous development amid the solitary struggles in the forest and the prairie." His movements were "unusually angular, even out West," but anyone who had heard that he "lived in the 'lowest hoosier style'" would be pleasantly surprised by his urbanity.

Though his early life had been "passed in the roughest kind of experience on the frontier," he had the strength of character to eschew the frontiersman's vices of tobacco and whiskey. A campaign song summed up the matter in the line: "Then, hurrah, boys for honest 'Old Abe of the West!' "[30]

Thus the Republican imagemakers of that time undertook to present their candidate as a typical and yet exceptional product of the Midwestern frontier. In doing so, they needed only to paint the man essentially as was. "I have urged Lincoln to act *himself*," one of them, John Andrew, wrote to another, Charles Ray, between the election and the inauguration. "I have also urged that he . . . should still be seen to be *characteristically* as a *Western* man: that the enterprise, bravery, frankness and simplicity supposed to belong to hardy volunteers in the great conquest over nature which are the supposed characteristics of pioneer life & manners among the best classes, are just the quality the people have bargained for."[31]

If the political principles of Lincoln were not peculiarly Southern when he was a Clay Whig in the 1840's, they were still less so after he became a Free-Soil Whig and then a Republican in the 1850's. In his speeches now it was repeatedly "we of the North," as opposed to "you of the South." He once said, "I think I have no prejudice against the Southern people" — but he never said that he was one of them, or that he agreed with them on the major questions of the day. Southerners insisted that their slaves were better off than the free workers of the North. "What a mistaken view do these men have of Northern laborers!" Lincoln exclaimed. "The man who labored for another last year, this year labors for himself, and next year he will have others to labor for him." Property influenced Northern as well as Southern thinking, Lincoln admitted. "In this we do not assume that we are better than the people of the South." The "immense pecuniary interest" in slaves caused Southerners to demand proslavery policies from the federal government. Lacking that kind of interest, "we at the North view slavery as wrong" and "think that slaves are human beings; *men,* not property."[32]

As president, struggling to put down the rebellion, Lincoln did exhibit a fellow feeling with Southerners, but only with those who, he thought, shared his devotion to the Union cause. "There is much reason to believe," he told the first wartime session of Congress, "that the Union men are the majority in many, if not in every other one [except South Carolina], of the so-called seceded States." His concern lest he "alarm our Southern Union friends" was a reason he later gave for going slowly in regard to confiscation and emancipation. He showed a special appreciation for the "loyal regions of East Tennessee and western North Carolina," and he rejoiced in the military aid that came from Southerners, black as well as white. After the surrender of Vicksburg and the opening of the Mississippi, he thanked the Northwest and the Northeast, then added: "The Sunny South too, in more colors than one, also lent a hand."[33]

Quite different was his attitude toward the leaders of the Confederacy. To justify the arbitrary arrest of suspected rebel sympathizers, he said in 1863 that a number of men, "now occupying the very highest places in the rebel war service, were all within the power of the [federal] government since the rebellion began, and were nearly as well known to be traitors then as now. Unquestionably if we had seized and held them, the insurgent cause would be much weaker." He illustrated his point with "a few notable examples." Among the "traitors" he thought should have been arrested in advance he included General Robert E. Lee.[34]

Rumor had it that Lincoln as president sometimes exhibited rebel sympathies under the influence of his Kentucky-born wife and her pro-Confederate relatives. Yielding to the appeal of family affection, he did occasionally grant presidential favors to enemy in-laws. A widow of a Confederate brigadier, Mrs. Lincoln's half-sister Emilie Todd Helm, even stayed at the White House for a short time. But family importunities became a vexation to Lincoln, and both he and Mrs. Lincoln put a limit on compliance. In 1864, pretending to expose a scandal, newspapers accused him of giving a pass for another of Mrs. Lincoln's half-sisters, Mrs. White, to carry merchandise into the Confederacy. Lincoln explained to his cabinet what had really happened. He and his wife had declined to see Mrs. White, but he did send her an ordinary pass. "She sent it back with a request that she might take trunks without [their] being examined. The President refused. She then . . . talked 'secesh' at the hotel, and made application" twice again through go-betweens. The president told the second of these that "if Mrs. W. did not leave forthwith she might expect to find herself within twenty four hours in the Old Capitol Prison."[35]

When looking beyond the war to the future of the South, some of his fellow Republicans insinuated that Lincoln had the interests of the rebels at heart. In the 10 percent plan, which he announced in December 1863, he indicated his hope of rebuilding each of the seceded states around a nucleus of native Unionists. Prominent Radicals charged, in the Wade-Davis Manifesto, that he was angling for "the electoral votes of the rebel States" in the election of 1864. His second inaugural — "With malice toward none, with charity for all, with firmness in the right" — seemed to some Northerners to provide further evidence of a softening of heart. So did his last public address, in which he expressed his "hope of a righteous and speedy peace." His intentions were not entirely clear, however, and his words were qualified: "speedy" by "righteous," and "charity" by "firmness in the right."[36]

In any case, his statements on Reconstruction did not, as yet, give reassurance to Southerners or cause them to pin their hopes on him. In their minds Lincoln remained until the end, as he had been throughout the war, the personification of the enemy and hence the personification of evil. " 'Exult not over thine adversary,' " a North Carolina "secesh lady" wrote on learning of his death, "but if Booth intended to turn assassin why, Oh why, did he delay it for so long?" Indeed, from the time when, in the 1850's, Lincoln had first come to the attention of Southern newspapers, they had pictured him as a potentially dangerous man, one "all broke out" with the deadly disease of abolitionism. "Everywhere in the West," the *New Orleans Delta* reported in 1858, "antislavery leaders" were raising high the "black banner." Among them "somebody named Lincoln" was in the eyes of his followers "an unborn Samson of the Free Soilers."[37] To this paper's readers he was a hostile rather than a friendly figure, and he was of the West, not the South.

Did contemporary Southerners regard Lincoln as one of their fellows? "For the most part," James G. Randall himself conceded, "in his own day the obvious answer is in the negative."[38]

[3]

The images of Lincoln that appeared after his death were largely reflections of those that had existed while he was alive. But many of the reflections were badly distorted. The most remarkable change occurred in the South, where Lincoln, the region's supposed malefactor, was transformed into its potential benefactor. This led, in the North as well as the South, to a grotesque exaggeration of the Southern in him.

Distortion reached its extreme in his representation as a person who habitually thought of himself as a Southerner and frequently called himself one. Even Randall could discover no direct contemporary evidence of Lincoln's ever having done so. The only thing he found was the recollection of a man who said that, at a White House interview in 1864, he had protested Lincoln's use of the term "Cuffie" for Negro, and that Lincoln had replied: "I stand corrected, young man, but you know I am by birth a Southerner and in our section that term is applied without any idea of an offensive nature."[39] This recollection was put down in 1889, a quarter-century after the event it purported to describe and well after the rise of the Lincoln-the-Southerner myth. In the light of Lincoln's known utterances in the 1850's and 1860's, it seems highly unlikely that, at any time during that period, he referred to the South as his native section or to himself as a representative of it.

The misconception of Lincoln has resulted partly from reading the present into the past, from confusing a later *Zeitgeist* with an earlier one. Kentucky was commonly viewed as a Southern state in Randall's time (as it is today) but not necessarily in Lincoln's time and certainly not in his youth. It was a Western state when Henry Clay went there in the 1790's — to become "Harry of the West" — and so it remained for a long time. In the census it was classified with the "Northwest" as late as 1850. Meanwhile, all the trans-Appalachian area, both above and below the Ohio River, was commonly looked upon as constituting the West. Gradually it became divided, as the process of sectionalization went on, to separate the entire country as between North and South. Even in 1860, however, the process was far from complete.[40]

In peopling the lower counties of Ohio, Indiana, and Illinois, the large numbers of Virginians, Carolinians, and Kentuckians did not create an extension of the South. They did not, of course, take slaves with them; indeed, many of them made the move in order to get away from slavery. "Newcomers into a region readily take on the habits and interests of their new environment," as Henry C. Hubbart has pointed out. "Even southern born men and women living in the free West in the forties and fifties could not be called southerners; much less could the children and grandchildren of those who earlier had migrated from the South into the region, be so called." To say that these people were typically Southern in their dislike for free blacks is to overlook the fact that, as recent events remind us, negrophobia "is no more a southern or a western than an American attitude."[41]

Lincoln's father was one of those frontiersmen who moved on to a farther frontier. There were more than a thousand slaves in the Hardin County of Abraham's boyhood, but his parents owned none, and the Baptist church to which they belonged was strongly opposed to slaveholding. Whether because of religious conviction or because of resentment against the pretensions of wealthy slaveowners, Thomas Lincoln clearly disliked the institution when he chose to resettle in Indiana, which was about the enter the Union as a free state.[42] It is meaningless to argue that, either in Kentucky or in Indiana, Lincoln grew up under a "Southern" family influence.

In becoming a follower of Henry Clay, Lincoln joined the national Whig party, not a "brotherhood of Southern Whigs." He saw in Clay a champion of human freedom, economic progress, and national union. Clay's constituency included big businessmen of the Northeast as well as large planters of the Southeast. Clay gained his reputation as the great compromiser through his efforts to hold the sections together — and to make himself president.

When sectionalism destroyed the Whig party, the new Republican party absorbed the Northern Whigs. It also took over, and added to, the Whig principles of Henry Clay. Though now preoccupied with the slavery question, Lincoln did not forget what Gabor Boritt has happily termed "the economics of the American dream."[43] Lincoln stood, as did the Republican party, for individual opportunity, for technological advance, for the enlarged productivity of farms and factories — all with the encouragement of the federal government. He fully shared the ideas and ideals that were implied in the party slogan of "Free soil, free labor, free men." He was the very embodiment of the spirit of modernization that was coming to predominate in the North. This spirit was the antithesis of the traditionalism that more and more characterized the South.

Lincoln seemed unsure of the extent to which blacks were to participate in the country's future. Sometimes he allowed them only a rather narrow scope, as when he declared, in the Charleston, Illinois, debate with Douglas, that he was not in favor of making social or political equals of them. Southern white supremacists later seized upon that statement and used it, along with his advocacy of colonizing freed blacks abroad, to demonstrate that he, too, had been an uncompromising white supremacist. But his latter-day admirers in the South overlooked a great many other things he had said, both in the Douglas debates and on other occasions. For instance, in his 1857 speech denouncing the *Dred Scott* decision, he expressed his conviction that the authors of the Dec-

163

laration of Independence had "intended to include *all* men" when they said that all men are created equal and are endowed with certain unalienable rights. The authors "meant to set up a standard maxim for free society," an ideal for "all people of all colors everywhere."[44]

If Lincoln hesitated on the issue of human rights so that there is doubt as to exactly where he stood at particular times, there can be no doubt as to the direction in which he was moving over the years. Under the pressure of events, he tended to advocate the more and more immediate realization of the promise of equality, especially after the start of the war. Not he but his party foes, the Democrats, were the confirmed racists of the North. Not he but they were the true friends of the white supremacists in the South.

On the question of Reconstruction, the recent historians who emphasize his growing radicalism are much closer to the truth than were the older writers who portrayed him as the last-ditch opponent of the Radicals, the unchanging advocate of black inferiority, the reluctant destroyer of slavery but the willing preserver of a caste system. The recent historians are inaccurate, however, in their treatment of some of the details. At certain points they make Lincoln appear to have been farther advanced than the evidence warrants. They discover in the documents, as previous writers also did, what their own predispositions reveal.

One of the key documents is Lincoln's proclamation of December 1863 setting forth his 10 percent plan of Reconstruction. This plan, according to the newer view, made emancipation the "first prerequisite for restoration" of a seceded state.[45] In fact, it did no such thing. It required the prospective state-makers to swear to support all congressional acts and presidential proclamations with regard to slavery. As yet, no act of Congress or action of the president called for complete abolition. The Emancipation Proclamation exempted those parts of the Confederacy that the Union armies had already recovered — the only parts where state-making then could possibly begin. Lincoln heartily approved when, in 1864, the first reconstructed government, in Louisiana, provided for statewide emancipation. But the plan he had announced in 1863 did not require it.[46]

Soon the big issue was no longer emancipation but suffrage for the Southern blacks. The new free-state constitution of Louisiana did not enfranchise Louisiana Negroes, though it authorized the legislature to do so — an unlikely prospect in the circumstances. After a visit from a Louisiana black delegation, Lincoln confidentially suggested to Governor Michael Hahn the propriety of giving the vote to at least a few of the "colored people." Thus far the sources are clear.[47] Some recent historians think they find evidence that Lincoln was temporarily willing to compromise with the Radicals in Congress by demanding Negro suffrage for the rest of the South if they would admit Louisiana without it. One thing the record makes plain, however, is that Lincoln insisted on the elimination of the Negro suffrage provision from the proposed Reconstruction bill.[48]

In his last public address, on April 11, 1865, Lincoln once more insisted on the admission of Louisiana without suffrage for blacks, though he now stated publicly what he earlier had written privately: "I would myself prefer that it were now conferred on the very intelligent, and on those who serve our cause as soldiers." He still said nothing about Negro suffrage in the other states to be reconstructed. Nevertheless, historians of the Lincoln-the-Radical school have leapt to the inference that the speech "forecast a new approach to reconstruction, one that would include at least limited enfranchisement of blacks" in Louisiana and "perhaps in the South as a whole." Lincoln did conclude the address by saying he might soon "make some new announcement." Whether he was planning on any significant change no one can tell. His most recent interpreter concedes that his assassination a few days later "makes it impossible to know precisely what direction his proposed shift in policy might have taken."[49] More than that: it makes it impossible to know whether he was actually planning any shift in policy.

This uncertainty has left ample room for speculation among historians, novelists, and politicians ever since Lincoln's death. Consciously or not, they have manipulated his memory to suit their own necessities. Opponents as well as proponents of Radical Reconstruction tried to get Lincoln on their side. Post-Reconstruction advocates of the New South and of sectional harmony appealed to his name. So did turn-of-the-century Southerners who opposed a renewal of federal intervention and who sought to justify state laws and constitutional amendments disfranchising and subordinating blacks. Throughout the first half of the twentieth century the resulting image of Lincoln the pro-Southern conservative prevailed among writers and teachers of history, North as well as South. Then, as the renewed movement for civil rights gained momentum, sympathetic historians attempted to enlist Lincoln in this cause.

There was a kind of nobility in the once widely held conception of a Lincoln who, by combining in himself the best of both North and South, became the shining symbol of American nationality. Such a view, however, overlooks his basic Western element. More seriously, it implies an endorsement of reunion with reaction, of nationalism revitalized at the expense of racial justice. We can discover in Lincoln a symbolism yet more noble, one that is both true to the record of the past and relevant to the needs of our own time. Whether or not his Western background made him a frontier type, it hardly made him the typical American of his day, to say nothing of ours. Nevertheless, in his political career he did stand — and in our memory he still may stand — for the kind of patriotism that calls for the removal of handicaps and the widening of opportunities for all people in all parts of the country and the world.

NOTES

1. J. G. Randall, *Lincoln and the South* (Baton Rouge: Louisiana State University Press, 1946), pp. 2-3, 6-7, 9, 11, 21-26, 50-53, 82-83, 119-23. This book comprises Randall's 1945 Fleming Lectures at Louisiana State University.

2. *New York Evening Post,* April 15, 1865, quoted in *Littell's Living Age* 85 (April 29, 1865): 188; Alexander H. Stephens, *A Constitutional View of the Late War between the States* (1868-70), and Jefferson Davis,

Rise and Fall of the Confederate Government (1881), cited in Michael Davis, *The Image of Lincoln in the South* (Knoxville: University of Tennessee Press, 1971), p. 112; J. G. deRoulhac Hamilton, "Lincoln and the South," *Sewanee Review* 17 (April 1909): 134-38. See also Hilary A. Herbert, *Why the Solid South?* (Baltimore: R. H. Woodward, 1890), p. 1, and Charles H. McCarthy, *Lincoln's Plan of Reconstruction* (New York: McClure, Phillips, 1901), p. 407.

3. Thomas Dixon, Jr., *The Clansman: An Historical Romance of the Ku Klux Klan* (New York: Doubleday, Page, 1905), p. 31. See also Davis, *Image of Lincoln,* pp. 150-51, and Roy P. Basler, *The Lincoln Legend: A Study in Changing Conceptions* (Boston: Houghton Mifflin, 1935), p. 240.

4. Ralph Waldo Emerson, "Abraham Lincoln: Remarks at the Funeral Services of the President, in Concord [New Hampshire], April 19, 1865," *Littell's Living Age* 85 (May 13, 1865): 282-84; Basler, *Lincoln Legend,* pp. 234-35, 239, quoting Lowell and Whitman; Whitman in Allen T. Rice, ed., *Reminiscences of Abraham Lincoln by Distinguished Men of His Time* (New York: North American Review, 1888), p. 470; George Alfred Townsend in Osborn H. Oldroyd, ed., *The Lincoln Memorial: Album Immortelles* (New York: G. W. Carleton, 1883), p. 513, quoted in Randall, *Lincoln and the South,* pp. 3-4; Frederick Jackson Turner, "The Problem of the West," *Atlantic Monthly* (September 1896), and "The Ohio Valley in American History" (an address to the Ohio Valley Historical Association, October 16, 1909), both in Turner, *The Frontier in American History* (New York: Holt, 1920), pp. 173-75, 217.

5. Emerson, "Lincoln," p. 283; Lowell in Basler, *Lincoln Legend,* p. 240; Turner, *Frontier in American History,* pp. 173-75; Henry W. Grady, *The New South and Other Addresses* ([1904] New York: Haskell House, 1969), pp. 27-28; Hamilton, "Lincoln and the South," pp. 130,137.

6. Lord Charnwood, *Abraham Lincoln* (New York: Holt, 1917), pp. 61, 454-55.

7. Thomas L. Connelly, *The Marble Man: Robert E. Lee and His Image in American Society* (New York: Knopf, 1977), pp. 99, 120-21.

8. Hamilton, "Lincoln and the South," pp. 133-34; Grover C. Hall, "We Southerners," *Scribner's Magazine* 83 (January 1928): 82; Archibald Rutledge, "A Southerner Views Lincoln," *Scribner's Magazine* 83 (February 1928): 204-7, 213, and "Lincoln and the Theory of Secession," *South Atlantic Quarterly* 41 (October 1942): 375; Robert L. Kincaid, "Lincoln and the Loyal South," *Vital Speeches of the Day* 15 (February 15, 1949): 269-73. See also Paul H. Buck, *The Road to Reunion, 1865-1900* (Boston: Little, Brown, 1937), pp. 254-55. In a debate at the 1930 convention of the American Historical Association the Southerner J. G. deRoulhac Hamilton described Lincoln as, by 1860, an antislavery radical. The Northerner Arthur C. Cole defended him as "Kentucky born and an Illinoisian by grace of the Westward movement" who "condemned abolition fanaticism." Cole and Hamilton, "Lincoln's Election

an Immediate Menace to Slavery in the States?" *American Historical Review* 36 (July 1931): 740, and 37 (July 1932): 703. A few decades later Lincoln's Northern defenders were to stress his radicalism rather than his conservatism.

9. David Donald, *Lincoln Reconsidered: Essays in the Civil War Era* (New York: Knopf, 1956), pp. 124-25.

10. The Wadsworth letter appears in Roy P. Basler, Marion Dolores Pratt, and Lloyd A. Dunlap, eds., *The Collected Works of Abraham Lincoln* (New Brunswick, N.J.: Rutgers University Press, 1953-55), 7:101-2. The editors considered it genuine.

11. Ludwell H. Johnson, "Lincoln and Equal Rights: The Authenticity of the Wadsworth Letter," *Journal of Southern History* 32 (February 1966): 83-87; Harold M. Hyman, "Lincoln and Equal Rights for Negroes: The Irrelevancy of the 'Wadsworth Letter,'" and Ludwell H. Johnson, "Lincoln and Civil Rights: A Reply," *Civil War History* 12 (September 1966): 258-66, and 13 (March 1867): 66-73. Johnson explains (*Journal of Southern History,* p. 87) that Horace Greeley's *New York Tribune* slogan in 1865 was "Universal Amnesty and Impartial Suffrage." He suggests that "the Marquis de Chambrun's *Scribner's* article was merely his inaccurate summary of the letter which appeared in the *Tribune* and other newspapers." Johnson perhaps concedes too much in accepting as probably genuine the passage in which Lincoln purportedly refers to "exacting" universal suffrage. Johnson admits (*Civil War History,* p. 73) that "had he lived, Lincoln doubtless would have moved, as the political center of balance moved, even further toward the Radical position on the Negro."

12. Hans L. Trefousse, *The Radical Republicans: Lincoln's Vanguard for Racial Justice* (New York: Knopf, 1969), pp. 286, 301.

13. Lincoln to Solomon Lincoln, March 6, 1848; to David Lincoln, April 2, 1848; to Richard V. B. Lincoln, April 6, 1860; and to John Chrisman, September 21, 1860, in Lincoln, *Collected Works,* 1:455-56, 461-62, 4:37, 117.

14. Lincoln to Jesse W. Fell, December 20, 1859, enclosing an autobiographical sketch; autobiography written for John L. Scripps [ca. June 1860], ibid., 3:511, 4:60-67; Jay Monaghan, *The Man Who Elected Lincoln* (Indianapolis: Bobbs-Merrill, 1956), p. 140, quoting the *Chicago Press and Tribune,* February 16, 1860; David W. Bartlett, *Life and Public Services of Hon. Abraham Lincoln* (New York: H. Dayton, 1860), p. 13.

15. Turner, *Frontier in American History,* p. 50, citing Massachusetts Historical Society *Proceedings* 42:73; Bartlett, *Lincoln,* p. 143; Goldwin Smith, "President Lincoln," *Littell's Living Age* 84 (March 4, 1865): 426.

16. According to a later recollection of William H. Herndon, he had heard Lincoln say, in 1850 or 1851, that his "mother was a bastard, was the daughter of a nobleman so called of Virginia," and that he himself had inherited his qualities of mind from that Virginia gentleman (Paul

M. Angle, ed., *Herndon's Life of Lincoln* [Cleveland: World, 1949], pp. 2-3). This book was originally published as William H. Herndon and Jesse W. Weik, *Herndon's Lincoln: The True Story of a Great Life* (Chicago: Belford, Clark, 1889). The recollection is one of many of Herndon's that lack credibility.

17. Ray to Washburn, December 24, 1854, quoted in Monaghan, *Man Who Elected Lincoln*, p. 41.

18. Quoted by Cole, "Lincoln's Election," p. 745.

19. Bartlett, *Lincoln*, pp. 25-26; Lincoln, *Collected Works*, 2:122. In his eulogy Lincoln here was quoting, with approval, from an unnamed newspaper.

20. Lincoln, *Collected Works*, 2:320.

21. Ibid., 3:440-41, 446.

22. Ibid., 4:70, 96-99.

23. Ibid., 4:198-99, 200, 426-27.

24. Ibid., 4:428.

25. Autobiography written for Scripps [June 1860]; Lincoln to Andrew Johnson, April 18, 1846, ibid., 1:377-79, 4:61-62.

26. Ibid., 3:463, 4:130-31.

27. Ibid., 4:190.

28. Ibid., 3:135, 140-41.

29. *Chicago Press and Tribune*, August 13, 1859, quoted in Monaghan, *Man Who Elected Lincoln*, p. 133.

30. Bartlett, *Lincoln*, pp. 106, 146-50.

31. John A. Andrew to Charles Ray, January 23, 1861, quoted in Monaghan, *Man Who Elected Lincoln*, p. 216. An Englishman, having visited Lincoln in the White House just after the 1864 election, recognized in him "the humour of the West" and refuted the charge of some English journals that he was a "brutal boor" — despite the "undeniable fact that he was the son of a poor Western farmer" (Goldwin Smith, "President Lincoln," 426-27).

32. Speeches at Bloomington, Illinois, September 12, 1854; Peoria, Illinois, October 16, 1854; Kalamazoo, Michigan, August 27, 1856; Hartford, Connecticut, March 6, 1860, in Lincoln, *Collected Works*, 2:230, 255, 264, 364, 4:3, 16. The *Council Bluffs Bugle*, August 17, 1859, reported Lincoln as saying in a speech there on August 13 that "he was willing to run for president in 1860, a Southern man with Northern principles, or in other words, with Abolition proclivities" (ibid., 3:396). Obviously the *Bugle*, a hostile Democratic paper, was putting words in his mouth.

33. Message to Congress, July 4, 1861; Lincoln to John C. Frémont, September 2, 1861; message to Congress, December 3, 1861; Lincoln to James C. Conkling, August 26, 1863, ibid., 4:437, 506, 5:36-37, 6:409.

34. Lincoln to Erastus Corning et al., [June 12,] 1863, ibid., 6:263, 265.

35. Howard K. Beale, ed., *Diary of Gideon Welles, Secretary of the Navy under Lincoln and Johnson* (New York: Norton, 1960), 2:21.

36. The Wade-Davis Manifesto was published in the *New York Tribune,* August 5, 1864, and later in other newspapers, and is conveniently reprinted in Henry S. Commager, ed., *Documents of American History,* 5th ed. (New York: Appleton-Century-Crofts, 1949), 1:439-40. The second inaugural and the last public address are in Lincoln, *Collected Works,* 8:332-33, 403-4.

37. Beth G. Crabtree and James W. Patton, eds., *"Journal of a Secesh Lady": The Diary of Catherine Ann Devereux Edmondston, 1860-1866* (Raleigh: North Carolina Division of Archives and History, 1979), p. 702; Davis, *Image of Lincoln,* passim; Albert J. Beveridge, *Abraham Lincoln, 1809-1858* (Boston: Houghton Mifflin, 1928), 2:384; *New Orleans Delta,* quoted in the *Chicago Press and Tribune,* July 5, 1858, and in Monaghan, *Man Who Elected Lincoln,* p. 109.

38. Randall, *Lincoln and the South,* pp. 4-5.

39. J. G. Randall and Richard N. Current, *Lincoln the President: Last Full Measure* (New York: Dodd, Mead, 1955), pp. 319-20. Davis, *Image of Lincoln,* states: "In later years . . . it became fashionable to point to Lincoln as a Southern man; indeed, Lincoln not infrequently referred to himself as such" (p. 17). Davis gives no evidence or examples of Lincoln's ever having done so. Very likely he is merely echoing Randall's statement.

40. Turner, *Frontier in American History,* pp. 31-33, 237, 241.

41. Henry C. Hubbart, " 'Pro-Southern' Influences in the Free West, 1840-1865," *Mississippi Valley Historical Review* 20 (June 1933): 45-48.

42. Benjamin Quarles, *Lincoln and the Negro* (New York: Oxford University Press, 1962), p. 16.

43. Gabor Boritt, *Lincoln and the Economics of the American Dream* (Memphis: Memphis State University Press, 1978).

44. See the editor's introduction in Richard N. Current, ed., *The Political Thought of Abraham Lincoln* (Indianapolis: Bobbs-Merrill, 1967), pp. xiii-xxix, especially p. xxi.

45. Peyton McCrary, *Abraham Lincoln and Reconstruction: The Louisiana Experiment* (Princeton: Princeton University Press, 1978), p. 188. McCrary cites Herman Belz, who in his *Reconstructing the Union: Theory and Practice During the Civil War* (Ithaca: Cornell University Press, 1969), pp. 162, 170, says that Lincoln's proclamation of December 1863 meant he "had committed himself to emancipation as the basis of reconstruction." Randall himself had written that, under Lincoln's December 1863 plan, the "loyal nucleus" should "establish a state government with abolition of slavery," though Randall drew from this no inference of radicalism on Lincoln's part (*The Civil War and Reconstruction* [Boston: Heath, 1937], p. 699). Following Randall, I have made the same error in the past. See Richard N. Current, *The Lincoln Nobody Knows* (New York: McGraw-Hill, 1958), p. 239.

46. For Lincoln's December 8, 1863, message and proclamation, see Lincoln, *Collected Works,* 7:50-55. Trefousse, *Radical Republicans,* p. 283, correctly observes: "But as yet he did not ask for abolition of slavery in areas where the Emancipation Proclamation did not apply — an omission that was bound to irk the ultras." McCrary himself at times recognizes the limits of the Emancipation Proclamation, as when he notes (*Lincoln and Reconstruction,* pp. 113-14) that it "would exempt southern Louisiana" and "left slavery intact on the lower Mississippi."

47. Lincoln to Michael Hahn, March 13, 1864, in Lincoln, *Collected Works,* 7:243. See also Benjamin Quarles, *The Negro in the Civil War* (Boston: Little, Brown, 1953), p. 251.

48. McCrary, *Lincoln and Reconstruction,* pp. 271, 288-89, 351. See also James M. McPherson, *The Struggle for Equality: Abolitionists and the Negro in the Civil War and Reconstruction* (Princeton: Princeton University Press, 1964), pp. 308-9; Belz, *Reconstructing the Union,* pp. 246-52; and David Donald, *Charles Sumner and the Rights of Man* (New York: Knopf, 1970), pp. 195-96.

49. McCrary, *Lincoln and Reconstruction,* pp. 304, 351. Lincoln's address of April 11, 1865, is in Lincoln, *Collected Works,* 8:403-4. The most persuasive case for Lincoln as an actual and potential champion of Negro rights is to be found in LaWanda Cox, *Lincoln and Black Freedom: A Study in Presidential Leadership* (Columbia: University of South Carolina Press, 1981).

⟦ XI ⟧

Bancroft's Lincoln

IT WAS TO BE the very first public observance of Abraham Lincoln's birthday. Promptly at noon on Monday, February 12, 1866, the House of Representatives met. The speaker's desk was draped in mournful black, and so was the clerk's, which the orator of the day was to occupy. At ten after twelve the senators began to file in, and following them the President of the United States, the designated orator, and the invited guests: Supreme Court justices, department heads and other government officials, foreign diplomats, army and navy officers, and state governors. Once all were in their places, a sound of dirges came from the vestibule, where the Marine Band was playing.

At half past twelve the president pro tem of the Senate called the two houses to order. Then the House chaplain offered a prayer, in which he touched upon the very theme that the orator of the occasion was to elaborate. "We worship thee as the God of our fathers," the chaplain intoned. "Thou didst trace for them a path over the trackless sea, and bring them to these shores, bearing with them the seed of a great dominion." The God of our fathers had not only founded but also sustained and preserved the nation. He had given the country Lincoln, had disciplined him "till the mere

A paper presented at a joint session of the Southeast American Studies Association and the South Atlantic Modern Language Association, Atlanta, Georgia, November 11, 1982. Here published for the first time.

172

politician was overshadowed by the nobler growth of his moral and spiritual nature," and had inspired him to free the slaves. "The Lord gave and the Lord hath taken away." The Lord gave again when he did "provide for that perilous moment one whose strength was sufficient to receive and bear the weight of government" — Andrew Johnson.

Next, the president pro tem of the Senate announced: "An eminent citizen, distinguished by his labors and services in high and responsible public positions at home and abroad — whose pen has instructed the present age in the history of his country, and done much to transmit the fame and renown of that country to future ages — Hon. George Bancroft — will now deliver a discourse." Warm applause greeted Bancroft as he took his place at the clerk's desk.[1]

He had not been the first choice of the joint congressional committee making arrangements for this affair. Originally the committee had invited Edwin M. Stanton, formerly Lincoln's and now Johnson's secretary of war, but Stanton had declined on the grounds of poor health. Whether or not Stanton would have been ideal, Bancroft in retrospect was certainly less than perfect for the assignment. True, he was the nation's preeminent historian, and at sixty-five he was still vigorous both physically and mentally. He was also an experienced politician, one who might have been expected to possess special insight into the conduct of a fellow politician. But Bancroft, a lifelong Democrat, had shown little or no sympathy with or appreciation of Lincoln while that Whig-Republican was alive. And Bancroft had a conception of history that, in itself, was perhaps more a hindrance than a help to a true understanding of Lincoln.

Bancroft had derived his conception of history partly from his father, a Congregationalist and then a Unitarian preacher, and partly from German thinkers such as G. W. F. Hegel and Leopold von Ranke, under whom he had studied at Göttingen and Berlin after graduating from Harvard. The Germans saw in the historical process the gradual realization of an idea — specifically, the idea of a unified and independent Germany. Bancroft focused on the idea of freedom and union as it materialized in America and, prospectively, throughout the world. He discovered something the Germans had overlooked, a guiding and controlling Providence, one that laid down the plan to which human events ultimately had to conform. Not that he expected this Providence to operate by means of miracles — not at all, for he considered himself a practitioner of "historical skepticism," an "objective" scholar, and he sought to establish his facts through the critical study of contemporary sources. No; his Providence intervened through natural (that is, divine) laws, through the universal mind, through the common people who partook of that mind, through the great men who embodied the idea and represented the people.[2]

Such — to put them sketchily and hence inexactly — were the convictions with which Bancroft had set out to write the history of the United States from the discovery of America to his own time. By 1866 he had published eight volumes and had carried the story down to the middle of the Revolutionary War. Eventually, in a tenth volume, he was to bring the narrative to 1782 and, in two more volumes, to the establishment of the new government under the Constitution. He was never to extend the history into his own lifetime, but he was ready, in his Lincoln address, to outline the intepretation he would have applied to the period from the founding of the republic to the end of the Civil War.

In his published volumes he had made clear who were the heroes and who the villains of American history. Good were the leaders who encouraged the colonies to stick together, to set up their own central authority, and to achieve national independence. Evil were the men who stood in the way. The great man lived close to nature and, from it, learned the lessons that enabled him to represent the people, to personify the national character, and to do the historic work of God. The greatest was, of course, George Washington. "At sixteen," Bancroft related, Washington "went into the wilderness as a surveyor, and for three years continued the pursuit, where the forests trained him, in meditative solitude, to

174

freedom and largeness of mind; and nature revealed to him her obedience to serene and silent laws." From this experience Washington gained "a divine and animating virtue."[3]

When Bancroft's first volume appeared, Andrew Jackson was president, and though the book dealt with the remote years 1492-1660 it seemed to endorse Jacksonian Democracy. The author, something of a rebel among the Massachusetts Brahmins, belonged to the Jacksonian party while nearly all the rest joined the more respectable Whigs. From Jackson's hand-picked successor, Martin Van Buren, he accepted a federal job as collector of the port of Boston. Wielding the collector's patronage, he made himself the state boss of the Democrats. He helped to bring about James K. Polk's nomination for the presidency and thus earned the position of navy secretary in the Polk administration (and later the honorific post of minister to England).

When Jackson died, in 1845, Bancroft qualified as the official eulogist not only by virtue of his scholarship but also by virtue of his status as a cabinet member, his devotion to the party, and his worship of the party's hero. In eulogizing Jackson he used the same standards of greatness as in characterizing Washington. Jackson, like Washington, was a child of nature who became the embodiment of the American spirit. The "inspired prophet of the West," Jackson was "like one of the mightiest forest trees of his own land, vigorous and colossal, sending its summit to the skies, and growing in its native soil in wild and inimitable magnificence, careless of beholders." He was "the representative, for his generation, of the American mind," for "by intuitive conception he shared and possessed all the creative ideas of his country and his time." Indeed, he *was* America.[4]

Though admiring Jackson and his inheritors Van Buren and Polk, Bancroft could muster little enthusiasm for the later Democratic Presidents Franklin Pierce and James Buchanan. These men were doughfaces, Northern men with Southern principles who allowed the Southern slaveholders to dominate the Democratic party. Bancroft was a Free-Soiler at heart, for he did not wish to see slavery spread into the territories of the West. When the Republican party emerged with a Free-Soil platform, Bancroft might have become a Republican, as many likeminded Northern Democrats did. Instead, he found in Stephen A. Douglas a Democratic leader whom he could follow and in Douglas's "popular sovereignty" (leaving the decision on slavery to the actual settlers of a territory) a principle that he could endorse. He voted for Douglas in 1860.

Bancroft feared the worst when Lincoln won the election. Several years earlier he had met him in Springfield and had seen nothing in him worth remembering. In 1861, as he watched him in the presidency, he gained little reassurance. Lincoln seemed to waver in dealing with secession and then to procrastinate in disposing of slavery, the real cause of disunion and the war. Bancroft confirmed his fears when he visited the nation's capital. "We suffer for want of an organising mind at the head of the government," he confided to his wife. "We have a president without brains." Drawing on his insight as a historian, he offered the brainless president some advice. "I sincerely wish to you the glory of perfect success," he wrote to him. "Civil War is the instrument of Divine Providence to root out social slavery." He secured an appointment with Lincoln to press the argument, only to hear from him the preposterous reply that slavery already had "received a mortal wound." Bancroft continued to worry about "the woes of our poor country," which "under incompetent hands" was "going fast to ruin."[5]

In 1862 Bancroft spoke to a group celebrating George Washington's Birthday at the Cooper Institute in New York. "The President of the United States has charged us," he said, "this day to meet and take counsel from the Farewell Address of Washington." The president himself, the speaker sarcastically declared, ought to take counsel from Washington's words. Bancroft was sounding so much like a Radical Republican that a Radical faction in New York City proposed to run him as a candidate for Congress. But he was unwilling to divide the Republican vote. The "people have chosen their President; and we who preferred another public servant must now consent to give vigour to the man who is President under the

Constitution," he replied. "Meantime, we cannot suffer the country to go to pieces because the President has committed errors."[6] Privately, he was less forgiving. Lincoln "is ignorant, self-willed, & is surrounded by men some of whom are almost as ignorant as himself," he told Francis Lieber. "How hard in order to sustain the country to sustain a man who is incompetent."[7]

In 1863, Lincoln having issued his final Emancipation Proclamation, Bancroft was prepared to think somewhat better of him. He was glad to comply when he received from him a request for historical information. Lincoln wanted to justify his suspension of the habeas corpus writ, and Bancroft responded with, of all things, a *British* precedent of 1776! He recommended that Lincoln get the "judgment of Congress" but assured him that his legal position was "perfectly safe without it."[8]

In 1864 the relations between the two grew increasingly cordial and, indeed, almost close. Invited to a Washington's Birthday reception at the White House, Bancroft recounted for his wife, with no more than a touch of condescension, the behavior of the president. "He took me by one of his hands, and trying to recall my name, he waved the other a foot and a half above his head, and cried out, greatly to the amusement of the by-standers: 'Hold on — I know you; you are — History, History of the United States — Mr. — Mr. Bancroft, Mr. George Bancroft,' and seemed disposed to give me a hearty welcome — expressing a wish to see me some day apart from the crowd." Bancroft, "finding him so good-natured," took advantage of the occasion to ask for an autographed copy of the Gettysburg Address, which he desired for a book of facsimiles he was putting together — *Autograph Leaves of Our Country's Authors*. Lincoln "very readily promised it," but when Bancroft later received the copy he found he could not use it, since, with writing on both sides, it could not properly be reproduced. So he asked Lincoln to write out the address anew, and Lincoln did, with a few corrections and revisions, thus producing what eventually came to be accepted as the standard text. That November, Bancroft voted for Lincoln's reelection.[9]

In early 1865 the two men, each unaware of what the other was doing, exerted themselves along parallel lines to push the Thirteenth Amendment through Congress. While Lincoln used patronage and persuasion on reluctant Democrats in general, Bancroft urged the logic of history upon one in particular, Representative Samuel S. Cox of New York. "Do away with slavery, and the Democrats will be borne into power on the wings of their sound principles of finance," he argued. "You know I have no fanaticism. I view this matter calmly, bringing out and applying the rules which history furnishes and which all are fixed and immutable as the laws of material progress."[10]

Then, after Lincoln's death, Bancroft had opportunities to restate for the public the lessons of history as these bore upon the moment. He was soon called upon to speak at a memorial mass meeting in Union Square, New York. After commending the late president — a man who, "scoffed at by the proud as unfit for his station," had "pursued a course of wisdom and kindness" — Bancroft concluded his remarks with a few words about the new president. Fortunately, Providence had put Andrew Johnson in the presidential chair, to complete the process of emancipation and "to consummate the vindication of the Union."[11]

Bancroft elaborated on "The Place of Abraham Lincoln in History" in an article that appeared in the June 1865 issue of the *Atlantic Monthly*. According to this article, Lincoln had taken office with few personal qualities that could enable him to meet the crisis he faced. He was "a man of defective education," "knowing nothing of administration," capable of speaking clearly "but not with eloquence," "unskilled in the use of the pen," and handicapped by a temperament that was "not suited to hardy action" but was "soft and gentle and yielding." Yet in some respects he was "peculiarly fitted for his task," since he was "one of the mass of the people; he represented them, because he was of them." As he "went along through his difficult journey," he "held fast by the hand of the people" and "was willing to take instruction from their wisdom." His place, "not in American history only, but in universal history," would depend on his proclamation of January 1, 1863. He "disclaimed all praise for the act" and gave the credit to God. Nevertheless, the consequence was that the country's "great principles of personal equality and freedom" would now "undulate through the world like the rays of light and heat from the sun."[12]

At the same time that Bancroft thus explained Lincoln's role, other Brahmins were presenting a similar interpretation, in part because they had read Bancroft's books and in larger part because they shared his transcendental view. "Surely, if ever there were an occasion when the heightened imagination of the historian might see Destiny visibly intervening in human affairs, here was a knot worthy of her shears." So wrote James Russell Lowell, and he no doubt was referring to the heightened imagination of the historian Bancroft. Like him, Lowell thought some higher influence would have had to make itself felt if the war were to be won under such a man as Lincoln, who took office "without experience and without reputation." It seemed to Lowell that the survival of the American system of government could be "directly traced to the virtue and intelligence of the people" and that "it was wise in Mr. Lincoln to leave the shaping of his policy to events."[13]

Ralph Waldo Emerson, though expressing a much more favorable opinion of Lincoln's character and competence, also agreed with Bancroft on the controlling hand of God. According to Emerson, the late president had by no means been lacking in eloquence of tongue or pen. Lincoln's "letters, messages and speeches" were "destined hereafter to wide fame." "His brief speech at Gettysburg will not easily be surpassed by words on any recorded occasion." "This man grew according to the need." He was "a man of the people," "thoroughly American," and with his fine qualities of "endurance . . . fertility of resources . . . magnanimity . . . courage . . . justice . . . humanity," he "stood a heroic figure in the centre of a heroic epoch." Still, he was but the agent of "a serene Providence which rules the fate of nations." "And what if it should turn out . . . that this heroic deliverer could no longer serve us . . . and what remained to be done required new and uncommitted hands . . . and that Heaven . . . shall make him serve his country even more by his death than by his life?"[14]

At first it appeared not only to Emerson and Bancroft but also to Radical Republican leaders in Congress that Johnson would act with the sternness that the times required and that Lincoln perhaps had lacked. Treason is a crime and crime must be punished, the new president was saying. But, once he had started his plan for restoring the seceded states, the Radicals began to look upon him as practically a traitor himself. He was now pardoning the rebel leaders and allowing them not only to retain power but also to maintain a form of slavery in disguise. By contrast, Senator Charles Sumner of Massachusetts was for assuring freedom to the former slaves by granting them the vote, and Representative Thaddeus Stevens of Pennsylvania was for making them independent farmers by giving them land, which he would obtain by confiscating the plantations of the former masters. Sumner said the Southern states, having committed suicide by seceding, were now but territories. Stevens said they were "conquered provinces." When Congress met in December 1865, the Republicans refused to admit the senators and representatives coming from the states that had reorganized under the Johnson plan.

While Bancroft's friend Sumner turned against Johnson, Bancroft himself remained loyal to him. He wrote to him soon after Lincoln's death to remind him they had met during the Polk administration and to assure him that the people were behind him now. This led to a frequent exchange of letters and eventually to an arrangement by which Bancroft composed the message that Johnson delivered to Congress soon after its assembly in December 1865 — a message that undertook to justify President Johnson's policy regarding the defeated South. Bancroft's service as Johnson's confidential adviser and ghostwriter was to remain a well-kept secret for more than forty years. If the Republicans in Congress had known of it in early 1866, they would never have selected Bancroft to deliver the memorial address on Lincoln's Birthday.[15]

So, inside the Capitol on February 12, 1866, Bancroft faced a badly divided audience, with respect to which he himself occupied a rather equivocal position. There, on the one hand, sat his friend Senator Sumner and the other Radicals, who by this time included the great majority of the Republicans in Congress. And there, on the other hand, sat President Johnson and his supporters in the legislative and executive branches, most of them Democrats. An open and bitter quarrel between the president and the congressional Republicans was about to break out, as they passed and he vetoed measures to protect the interests of black people in the South.

"Senators, Representatives of America," Bancroft now began. "That God rules in the affairs of men is as certain as any truth of physical science." The "immovable Omnipotence" sometimes "steps along mysterious ways," but "when the hour strikes for a people, or for mankind, to pass into a new form of being," an "all-subduing influence prepares the minds of men for the coming revolution," and "those who plan resistance find themselves in conflict with the will of Providence."[16] How well the recent history of the United States illustrated this truth!

"In the fullness of time a Republic rose up in the wilderness of America," Bancroft went on. From "whatever there was of good in the systems of former centuries she drew her nourishment," and "the vine of liberty took deep root and filled the land." "The fame of this only daughter of freedom went out into all the lands of the earth; from her the human race drew hope." Yet in this happy land there lurked a "false conception" of the kind that "portends disaster, shame, and death." That was slavery. "At the North the growth of slavery was arrested by natural causes; in the region nearest the Tropics it throve rankly." The original Democrats opposed its spread by means of the "Jefferson proviso" excluding it from the territories, a proviso that Jefferson incorporated in the Northwest Ordinance.[17]

Only after Bancroft had been speaking for half an hour did he get around to mentioning the man whom the occasion was in-

181

tended to honor. In 1860 the "choice of America fell" on a typically Bancroftian representative man. This one had grown up in an Indiana log cabin, "with the solemn solitude for his teacher in his meditative hours." He "lived the life of the American people, walked in its light, reasoned with its reason, thought with its power of thought, felt the beatings of its mighty heart, and so was in every way a child of nature, a child of the West, a child of America."

As president-elect, Lincoln showed that he understood the historical process intuitively. In his Springfield farewell, after saying George Washington "never would have succeeded except for the aid of Divine Providence," he declared: "On the same Almighty Being I place my reliance, without which I can not succeed, but with which success is certain." To the "men of Indiana" he confessed: "I am but an accidental, temporary instrument; it is your business to rise up and preserve the Union and liberty." At Albany, New York, he reaffirmed: "I must rely upon the people." In Philadelphia he added: "I have never had a feeling politically that did not spring from the sentiments embodied in the Declaration of Independence, which gave liberty, not alone to the people of this country, but to the world in all future time."[18]

On God and the people he did rely, once he was president and the war had come. The men of Indiana and the rest of the Northern states did rise up, and they "put forth such miracles of effort as the history of the world had never known." Lincoln did not lead but followed them. "The President was led along by the greatness of their self-sacrificing example; and as a child, in a dark night on a rugged way, catches hold of the hand of its father for guidance and support, he clung fast to the hand of the people, and moved calmly through the gloom." Apparently this child of nature was a child indeed. He practically had to be dragged to proclaiming emancipation, and he proclaimed it, after "vain resistance," only when he "at last saw that slavery must be abolished or the Republic must die."[19]

When, after an hour's discourse, Bancroft took up Lincoln's character, he gave the impression that Providence had done remarkably well to fashion such an effective instrument out of such unpromising material. Lincoln, the orator conceded, did have some attractive qualities. He was "the most unassuming of men," always willing to give credit where credit was due — "to those whom he employed, to the people, and to the providence of God." He was of "unblemished purity in private life, a good son, a kind husband, a most affectionate father, and, as a man, so gentle to all." He had "integrity." Douglas, his great rival, once remarked: "Lincoln was the honestest man I ever knew."

Yet, Bancroft indicated, despite his virtues as a person he had serious faults as a president. In the "habits of his mind" he was too much like Hamlet, too given to "meditation and inward thought," too slow and hesitant to act. He lagged so much behind public opinion that "the course of his Administration might have been explained as the calculating policy of a shrewd and watchful politician, had there not been seen behind it a fixedness of principle." His "sensibilities were not acute; he had no vividness of imagination to picture to his mind the horrors of the battlefield or the sufferings in hospitals." "In judging of character he failed in discrimination, and his appointments were sometimes bad." His "supervision of affairs was unsteady and incomplete, and sometimes, by a sudden interference transcending the usual forms, he rather confused than advanced the public business." If those traits amounted to something less than heroic, well, that is the way Lincoln was. Not he but "the American people was the hero of the war."[20]

Bancroft berated the wartime leaders of Great Britain for showing little sympathy with either Lincoln or the Union cause. Between the humble and democratic Lincoln and the arrogant and aristocratic Lord Palmerston he drew a contrast that denigrated the late prime minister more than it complimented the recent president.

Before concluding, after having read on for about an hour and a half, he had something to say about the pressing and divisive issue of the moment, the question of reconstructing the South.

Though he did not mention President Johnson, he more than hinted that he was on Johnson's side, and he implied that Lincoln, if alive, would be also. "It was the nature of Lincoln to forgive," and he was "eager to receive back his returning countrymen" of the South as soon as hostilities had ended. "Three days before his death he declared his preference that 'the elective franchise were now conferred on the very intelligent of the colored men and on those of them who served our cause as soldiers'; but he wished it done by the States themselves, and he never harbored the thought of exacting it from a new government as a condition of its recognition." To make Negro suffrage such a condition was what Sumner and other Republicans now wanted to do. "The States which have left us are not brought back as subjugated States," Bancroft added, "for then we should hold them only so long as that conquest could be maintained; they come to their rightful place under the Constitution as original, necessary, and inseparable members of the Union."[21] That was good Johnsonian doctrine.

Bancroft was satisfied that he had offered words to please the Radicals as well as the Johnsonites. While going along he had noticed — and he thought it the "drollest thing" — that at certain points "the radicals would applaud vigorously" and at others the friends of Johnson would do so. It "was like touching the different keys of a piano, each sounding its note at the touch."[22] Though most of the Republicans objected to Bancroft's implied endorsement of Johnson, none of them seemed to find anything objectionable in his unflattering treatment of Lincoln. Apparently they shared both the speaker's impression of Lincoln's character and the speaker's conception of the historic roles of Lincoln, the people, and God.

Yet, among official eulogies of American public figures, this must surely be one of the least eulogistic on record. Certainly Bancroft's portrayal of Lincoln was much less favorable than his portrayal of either Washington or Jackson. Each of the three was the representative man, the great man, of his own generation, in the historian's view. Each emerged from the American wilderness, personified the American character, and played a key part in the fulfillment of the American destiny. But Lincoln the human being comes across as much the least admirable, much the least heroic.

Bancroft and his fellow Brahmins contributed to forming the popular image of Lincoln that was to prevail for many years. In this picture the wartime president had little to do, as an agent in his own right, with the events of the Civil War. Except at the moment when, with a stroke of his pen, he struck the shackles from the slaves, he was merely a kind of brooding presence — or, more accurately, a kind of brooding absence — until the end, when he was planning exactly the Reconstruction policy that his successor tried to carry out. Later historians and biographers illuminated phases of the subject that were entirely dark to Bancroft and his contemporaries. Bancroft was quite unaware of the complexities of Lincoln's personality, his real concern for the rights of the freedmen, his conduct of the war in the role of commander-in-chief, or the way he made himself a statesman by behaving like a politician. The lack of attention to Lincoln's political skill is especially surprising in view of Bancroft's own experience with down-to-earth politics.

A true appreciation of Lincoln, or something approximating it, lay in the distant future as Bancroft concluded his address, waited for the benediction by the Senate chaplain, and then followed the senators and President Johnson out of the House chamber, ahead of the other invited guests, while the Marine Band played patriotic tunes.[23]

NOTES

1. Charles R. Cushman, ed., *Memorial Addresses Delivered before the Two Houses of Congress on the Life and Character of Abraham Lincoln, James A. Garfield, William McKinley* (Washington: Government Printing Office, 1903), pp. 79-97.

2. Russel B. Nye, *George Bancroft, Brahmin Rebel* (New York: Knopf, 1944), pp. 95-97. See also David Levin, *History as Romantic Art: Bancroft, Prescott, Motley, and Parkman* (Stanford: Stanford University Press, 1959), pp. 25-26, 38, 49-51, and Richard C. Vitzthum, *The American*

Compromise: Theme and Method in the Histories of Bancroft, Parkman, and Adams (Norman: University of Oklahoma Press, 1974), pp. 4-7, 14-16.

3. Levin, *History as Romantic Art*, p. 53; Vitzthum, *American Compromise*, p. 6.

4. Nye, *Bancroft*, pp. 116-19, 149-50.

5. Ibid., pp. 208-9; Bancroft to Mrs. Bancroft, September 1861, to Lincoln, November 1861, and to Mrs. Bancroft, December 16, 1861, in M. A. De Wolfe Howe, *The Life and Letters of George Bancroft* (New York: Scribner's, 1908), 2:132, 143n, 145.

6. Nye, *Bancroft*, pp. 216-17; Howe, *Life and Letters*, 2:151-52, 154.

7. Bancroft to Lieber, October 29, 1862, in Robert H. Canary, *George Bancroft* (New York: Twayne, 1974), pp. 100-101.

8. Howe, *Life and Letters*, 2:154-55; Nye, *Bancroft*, p. 220.

9. Howe, *Life and Letters*, 2:155-56; Nye, *Bancroft*, p. 220.

10. Bancroft to Cox, January 28, 1865, in Howe, *Life and Letters*, 2:157.

11. Nye, *Bancroft*, pp. 224-26.

12. George Bancroft, "The Place of Abraham Lincoln in History," *Atlantic Monthly* 15 (June 1865): 762-64.

13. James Russell Lowell, "Abraham Lincoln, 1865-1865," in *The Complete Writings of James Russell Lowell* (New York: AMS Press, 1966), 6:224-25, 251.

14. Ralph Waldo Emerson, "Abraham Lincoln: Remarks at the Funeral Services Held in Concord, April 19, 1865," in *The Complete Works of Ralph Waldo Emerson*, centenary edition, ed. Edward Waldo Emerson (Boston: Houghton Mifflin, 1911), 11:332-34, 336-37.

15. Nye, *Bancroft*, pp. 226-30. All students of Bancroft are indebted to Nye for this biography, which fully deserves the Pulitzer prize it was awarded. Nye is in error, though, in saying (p. 231) that "Bancroft's assistance in the preparation of Johnson's message undoubtedly led to his being chosen as the official eulogist of Lincoln." A congressional committee, not the president or his cabinet, chose the speaker for the occasion. The committee members did not know that Bancroft had ghostwritten the message; if they had known, the Republican majority could hardly have been expected to choose him.

16. Cushman, ed., *Memorial Addresses*, pp. 7-9.

17. Ibid., pp. 9-26.

18. Ibid., pp. 26-32.

19. Ibid., pp. 52-53, 57-58.

20. Ibid., pp. 65-69, 74.

21. Ibid., pp. 69-74.

22. Bancroft to Mrs. Bancroft, February 12, 1866, in Howe, *Life and Letters*, 2:159.

23. Cushman, ed., *Memorial Addresses*, pp. 97-98.

INDEX

∾

Note on the Author

BORN IN 1912 in Colorado City (now a part of Colorado Springs), Colorado, Richard Nelson Current received his B.A. from Oberlin College, his M.A. from the Fletcher School of Law and Diplomacy, and his Ph.D. from the University of Wisconsin (Madison). He has taught in colleges and universities from the Atlantic to the Pacific and from Lake Superior to the Southern Piedmont, among them the universities of Illinois (Urbana-Champaign), Wisconsin (Madison), and North Carolina (Greensboro). Besides serving as Harmsworth Professor at Oxford University and Fulbright Professor at the universities of Munich and Chile (Santiago), he has lectured on American history in Italy, Belgium, the Netherlands, Norway, Japan, India, Taiwan, the Philippines, Argentina, Ecuador, Australia, and Antarctica. He is the author of numerous articles and reviews and the author or co-author of seventeen books, four of them on Abraham Lincoln.

DATE DUE

DEMCO 38-297